Walks In and Around Ledbury
A Pictorial Guide To

Ledbury

An illustrated Study and Exploration of Ledbury and its Environs.

by Carl Flint FRSA

Published by Malvern Walks
Aldine Print Ltd
Barnards Green
Malvern
WR14 3NB

© Carl Flint 2017

First published in Great Britain 2017

ISBN 978-0-9566295-8-6

The right of Carl Flint to be identified as the author of this work has been asserted by him in accordance with the Copyright, Designs and Patent Act 1988

2 4 6 8 10 9 7 5 3 1

Published by Malvern Walks and printed in Great Britain by Orchard Press Cheltenham Ltd, Northway Trading Estate, Tewkesbury GL20 8JH

Author's Note

Walks In and Around Ledbury: A Pictorial Guide to Ledbury is presented in the Alfred Wainwright style. Black and white drawings with the Bradley Hand font seek to preserve the Gold Standard he set for all guide books. Each walk attempts to capture as much local history as is humanly possible to bring the walk to life with the echoes of the past. Whether it is deeply embedded musket ball from the English Civil War in the north door of the parish church or an unusual name on a cast iron wall plaque, they tell a story. I am indebted to the guide who many years ago took my wife and I on a Cadfael Walk around Shrewsbury town centre. The linkage with the historic buildings to the fictional Benedictine detective monk was superb and laid the foundation for me to attempt the same here.

I find carrying out the research to better understand the context or to double check a fact is an enjoyable and fascinating experience. For example the inscription on the blacksmiths grave stone in the churchyard of Ledbury Parish Church of St Michael and All Angels, is said to have inspired a line in John Masefield's narrative poem of 1911, 'The Everlasting Mercy'. Many of the guides available on the

Internet or in trusty paper format suggest that this witty epitaph is unique:

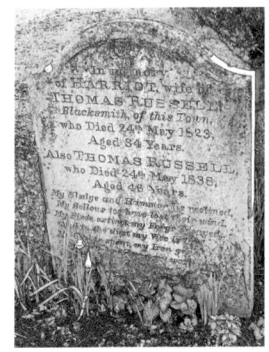

My sledge and hammer lie reclined,
My bellows too have lost their wind. My fire's extinct, my forge decayed, and in the dust my vice is laid.
My coal is spent, my iron gone.
My fire dried corpse now lies at rest.
My soul smoke-like is soaring to be blest

However further research has indicated that the same inscription can be found on George Jones village blacksmith gravestone, in Old Cleeve Churchyard, Somerset and further more with thanks to Jim Leonardson and The Quaint Epitaph's book. There is an undated gravestone in Norton, Massachusetts, USA which reads:

My sledge and hammer lie reclined,
My bellows too have lost their wind.
My fire's extinct, my forge decayed,
and in the dust my vice is laid.
My iron spent, my coal is gone.
My nails are drove — my work is done.

So, could the Ledbury epitaph be the original or was it copied? If you know then please email me at info@malvernwalks.co.uk

I have learnt through my previous books that circular walks are a prerequisite and the accessibility of refreshments en route is a key factor to a grand day out.

With the advent of mobile phone technology and the ease of communicating via the Internet, the book now includes 21st Century interactive technology in the form of QR codes. These link to sound and picture files I have recorded on YouTube and are saved to the 'Cloud'. With a quick scan of a mobile phone the YouTube file can be downloaded enabling you to hear the sound of me talking about a feature  which hopefully will enhance your experience of the walk. A kind of 'Talking Book' no less! For those not so caught up on the Internet, this book with its trusty paper pages will thankfully age like a good wine with time.

Although I am not a keen Facebook user, I have with the help of Joshua Flint created a Facebook page which describes my latest walking and writing activity. It is called 'Pictorial Guides of the Malvern Hills and Ledbury'. So please 'like me' (don't you just hate this terminology!).

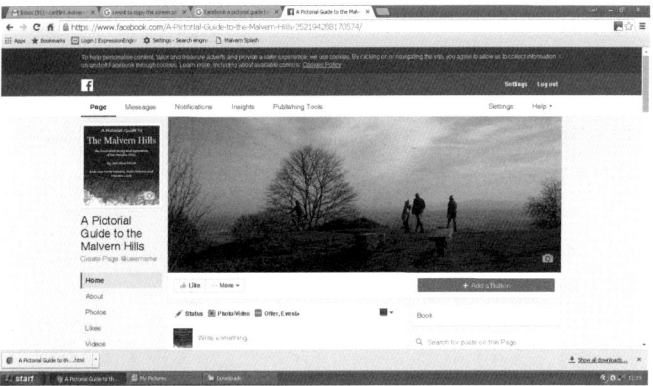

My email address is info@malvernwalks.co.uk and my website is www.malvernwalks.co.uk I can also be contacted via the Malvern Tourist Information Centre website.

This book will grow as later editions are published, hopefully enhanced by contributions from like-minded people. All submissions which help to improve the walks will be acknowledged on the website and in the following reprint. So thank you in advance! The Herefordshire and Worcestershire countryside is a large part of my life. I hope you get as much pleasure as I do from the walks.

Acknowledgements

Su Savage, freelance designer has been an inspiration from the beginning with her skilfully crafted design work, she has created a careful balance of text and imagery. After the first book was published I realised I could not carry on without a proof reader and luckily Justine Sissons came to my rescue. She has the skills which most of us do not possess, that is the ability to spot the smallest mistake. Many friends have also helped by checking out the walks and providing feedback. My route checkers are armed with just the text versions of the walks and if they find their way around the route without any problems, I then feel confident that someone new to the area should be able to comfortably follow the walk aided by the text, map and pictures.

New roads are built, footpaths 'disappear', boundaries change and hostelries can be 'under new management', all of which ensures this book is out of date before it is published. Any contributions and corrections forwarded to my email info@malvernwalks.co.uk will be published in the next edition along with the name of the contributor. Thank you in advance!

Contents

Chapter		Page
1	Introduction	9
2	Walk 1 Ledbury town centre Heritage Walk	20
3	Walk 2 Around Ledbury town: a brief history of transport in Ledbury	68
4	Walk 3 Ledbury town centre to Eastnor Castle circular walk	91

Waypoints	113
Hostelries close to Walks 1 to 3	114
Bibliography	121
Web Addresses	122
Contributors	123
Index	126

Chapter 1

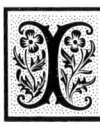ntroduction

'Walks In and Around Ledbury: A Pictorial Guide to Ledbury ' has been written for the rambler, tourist and where suitable joggers and the mountain biker to enjoy and experience the breathtaking splendour of the Herefordshire countryside.

Ledbury is a delightful English market town nestling in the undulating Herefordshire countryside. It is famed for its black and white buildings and literary heritage through Elizabeth Barrett Browning and John Masefield. For those visiting Ledbury for the first time the town has a prosperous and distinct feel about it. This is probably a combination of sensitive town planning and the abundance of local retailers rather than 'national chains' housed in old character premises. I believe a sure sign of upbeat 'localism' can be identified by the number of independent butchers on the High Street. Ledbury can boast three independent butchers whilst sadly neighbouring Great Malvern has none.

For those seeking out the local history Ledbury has a wealth of charming nooks and crannies to be explored thanks to the Bishop of Hereford who planned Ledbury's development with narrow plots of land called burgages. The Market House is the most prominent building on the High Street with its 16 sturdy oak pillars providing a covered market, supporting the original black and white timbered grain store. Standing beneath the Market House and looking towards Church Lane early in the morning you may find yourself transformed back in time to a Dickens classic. Turning back to the High Street across the road is the imposing Victorian built Elizabeth Barrett Browning Institute, to the left are the almshouses of St. Katherine's Hospital and then the most spectacular display of black and white timbered buildings to grace any town culminating in the Feathers Hotel, the House on Stilts and Ledbury Park by the crossroads.

There are three walks in this book which attempt to capture the history, architecture, culture and as always the unusual and the different that this fascinating town and countryside has to offer.

Getting There

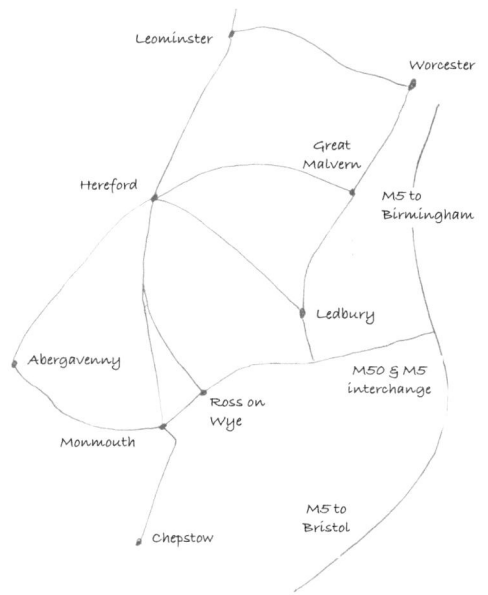

The principal routes into Ledbury are via Junction 2 of the M50 which provides access to the south and east side of the town via the A447. This road also serves as a bypass to the south of the town leading to the Hereford Road, the A417. The undulating but direct route to Ross on Wye via the A449 passes the Rugby Club and nature reserve next to the River Leadon. The A449 continues north to British Camp and the Malverns. If approaching Ledbury from Malvern a one-way system operates at the central crossroads which means a left hand turn is advisable if attempting to head to Ross on Wye or the motorway.

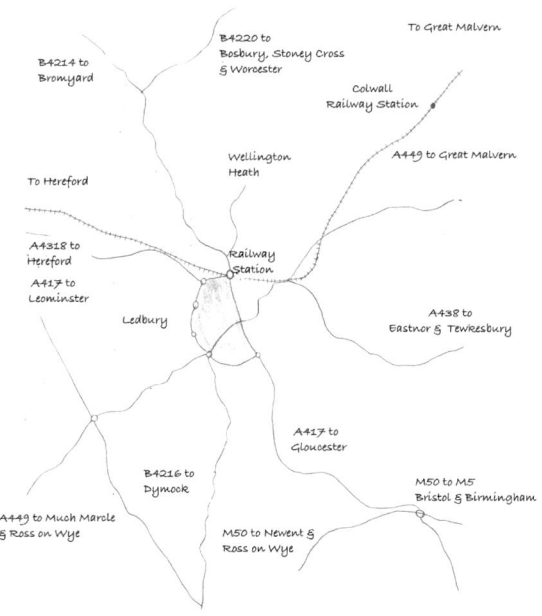

Trains to Hereford to access Wales and to Worcester and London are provided by Great Western Railways (GWR) 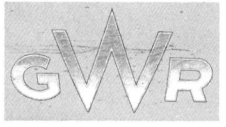 with five direct trains to and from London each day and a further ten trains with connecting services (London Midland) either at Great

Malvern or Worcester. However, be prepared to wait up to an hour for connecting services.

London Midland provides the service between Hereford and Birmingham via Worcester on an hourly basis.

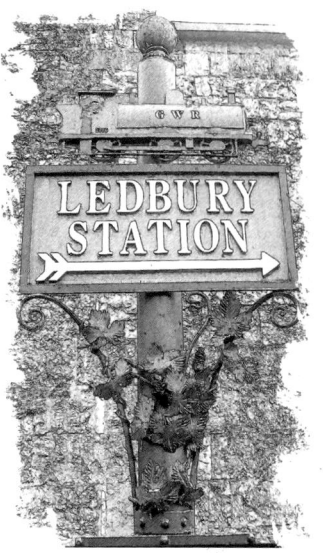

For GWR tickets and travel information visit www.gwr.com or call 03457 000125. For National Rail Enquiries visit www.nationalrail.co.uk or telephone 08457 484950.

Bus services

There are only two bus routes to and from Ledbury providing an hourly service, the 132 provided by Stagecoach to Newent and Gloucester and the 675 to Colwall and Great Malvern provided by Astons. There are another ten bus routes, with some providing less than five journeys per day, or operating on market days or just in the summer months. The Herefordshire Council provides a bus route map and travel information for the County and is available from the tourist information centre or the Hereford move website. See www.herefordmove.org

Coach travel is provided by National Express service 445 to Heathrow Airport and Victoria Coach Station and stops outside the Market House at roughly two hourly intervals during the morning. Strangely there is only one return journey per day, arriving back late in the evening.

Cycle hire is available from the Ledbury Cycle Hire, Old Kennels Farm, Bromyard Road, HR8 1LG. From Ledbury station head down onto the Homend and turn right under the railway bridge and along the Bromyard Road for 300m.

Reference to other supporting materials to make a visit more enjoyable.

Ledbury appears on the far edge of the Ordnance Survey maps. The Landranger series 149 has a scale of 1:50,000, and gives a good overview of the area but Ledbury town is tucked into the last few squares of the Eastings on the extreme right. The Ordnance Survey Explorer Map 190, Malvern Hills & Bredon Hill, gives the level of detail necessary to discover the nooks and crannies but the town is literally cut off by the first Easting with the A417 going over the map boundary.

The 189 Hereford & Ross-on Wye OS Explorer map covers the area west of Ledbury and very usefully the Wye Valley, Hereford and down to Ross on Wye. The scale is 1:25,000, which equates to 4 cm to 1 km (2½ inches to 1 mile in old currency). My latest OS map purchase includes a free digital map download to my phone (my daughter's hand-me-down), which is fine when you have an Internet connection, otherwise it is the paper version when out in the countryside.

Ledbury is blessed with not one but two cavernous bookshops, The Three Counties Bookshop (telephone 01531 635699) and Ledbury Books and Maps (telephone 01531 633226). It is easy to see how these two bookshops prosper on this small High Street as they each have quite a unique identity.

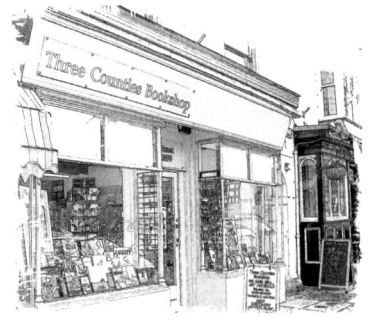

Sadly since my first excursion to Ledbury, the Tourist Information Centre (TIC) has moved out of the Masters House and into the recesses of the Ice Bytes Internet Cafe on the Homend. Whilst the cafe is positively lovely serving great food and beverages the TIC is unstaffed and merely consists of a couple of shelves of leaflets. This is very sad when one considers how successful the TIC's are in Malvern and Worcester.

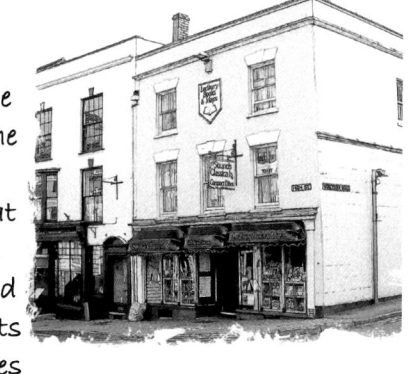

Further afield, 'The Map Shop' in Upton upon Severn is renowned countywide for providing a comprehensive range of maps and books of local and international interest. It is of course now possible to specify and buy a map where Ledbury is located in the centre, which would be a very wise move. Contact details for the Map Shop are:
- 15 High Street, Upton upon Severn, WR8 0HJ. Telephone 0800 0854080. They are open Monday to Saturday 9.00a.m to 5.30pm.

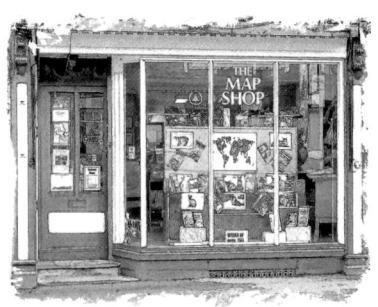

Worcester has a large Waterstones to browse through and is located in The Shambles. The TIC stocks a wide range of guide books and is located next to the historic Guildhall which is well worth a visit. The highly recommended historic town centre walk leaves at 11.00 am most mornings and offers a fascinating insight into the history of Worcester and its role in the English Civil War, circa 1651.

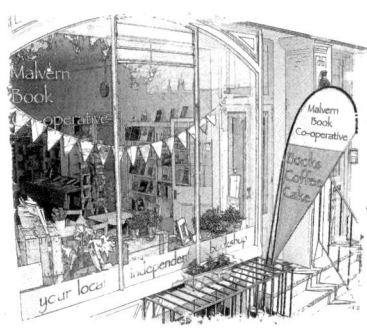

Neighbouring Great Malvern has the Malvern Book Cooperative just a few paces up in St Anns Road. They are open Monday to Saturday 9.30a.m to 5.30pm. Telephone 01684 564788.

Many of the drawings printed throughout the book are either drawn by myself or digitally generated using Akvis software.

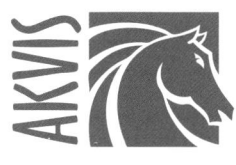

This specialist software package converts photographs into a black and white line drawing style. I trust that the combination of these images and commentary begin to recreate on paper what is so enchanting about Ledbury.

Markets

Market days are Tuesday and Saturday underneath the Market House. The Tuesday Market is known as the Ledbury Market Charter going back 1138 when King Stephen issued a charter to Bishop Robert de Bethune. The Farmers Market is held on the last Friday of the month.

Festivals

The Ledbury Poetry Festival. This takes place during the first ten days of July. There are readings, films, a new writers programme and of course huge school involvement. On the last Saturday of the festival it broadens out into local food and drink produce. For more information see: www.poetry-festival.co.uk/
The Ledbury Mop Fair is held on a Monday and Tuesday in mid-October in the High Street, the lower section of the Homend and Bye Street. It has its roots in medieval times.

Originally a Mop Fair was for hiring workers and dates back to Edward III who wanted to regulate the labour market at a time of shortage after the Black Death. Workers would attend the

Mop Fair dressed in their best clothes and carry an item signifying their trade. A tassel or mop was worn on the lapel and indicated they were for hire. If they gained new employment the mop was removed and replaced with ribbons. Today the fair is of the roller coaster, dodgem car genre.

The Lakefest music festival takes place in the Eastnor Castle Deer Park during mid-August. For further information see: http://www.efestivals.co.uk/festivals/lakefest/2017/ Eastnor Castle Chilli Festival is held on the May Bank Holiday weekend and is a very popular event.

The Market Theatre is in Market Street just a short way down Bye Street. It opened in 2000 and provides a venue for live shows and cinema. Telephone 01531 63376.

Chapter 2

Walk 1

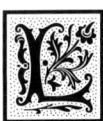 edbury town centre Heritage Walk

Summary

This circular walk around Ledbury uncovers the considerable heritage Ledbury has to offer. The walk will delve into nooks, crannies and alleyways not often observed for which Ledbury has in abundance. Although the distance covered is not great, it will be impossible just to walk this route without recourse to absorbing and reflecting on the architecture and history that is just around each corner. So be prepared to spend two hours and quite possibly up to three hours undertaking this fascinating walk.

There are refreshments a plenty.

No springs, wells or spouts just a diverted stream behind the churchyard.

No stiles or swing gates, it is all on pavements.

Connections to other walks
Walk 2 Around Ledbury Town: a brief history of transport in Ledbury.

Walk 3 Ledbury to Eastnor Castle circular walk.

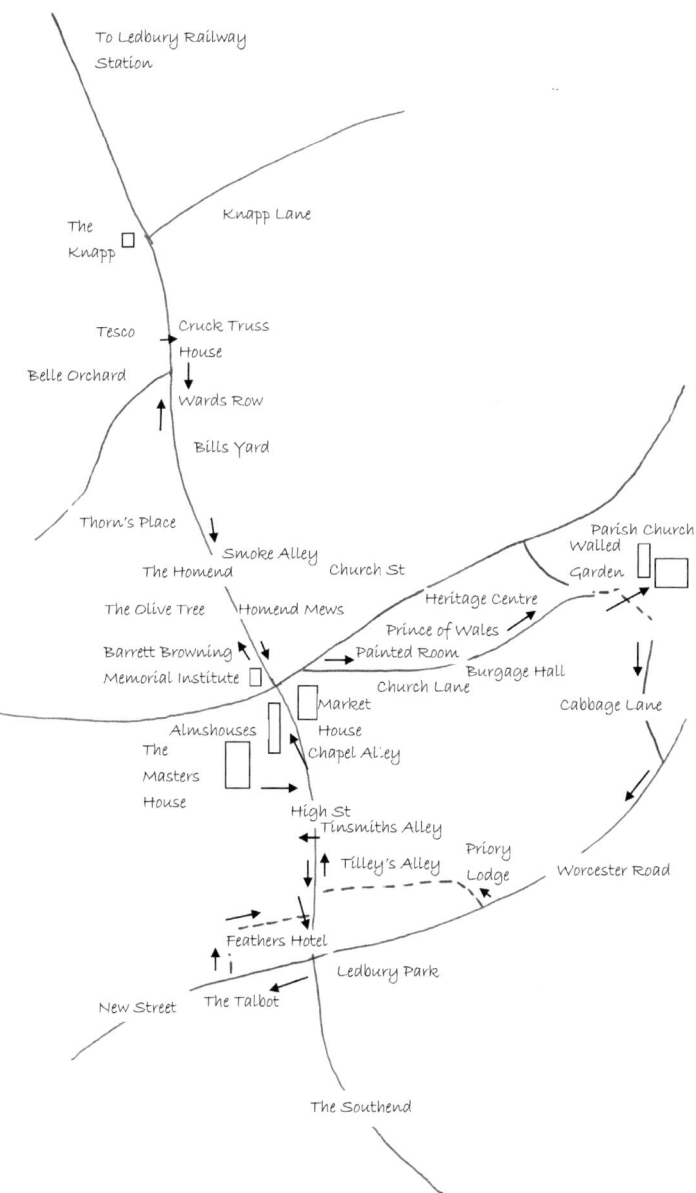

The walk

The walk can be started at any convenient point. So if arriving by car it is probably best to park in St Katherine's car park which is the main town centre pay and display car park next to St Katherine's Hospital and the Master's House.

Although this area is referred to in historical guides as St Katherine's Hospital, the modern-day focal point is the Masters House. So begin by going into the Master's House which is open from 9.30am to 4.30pm weekdays except Wednesday when it is closed and 9.30am to 12.30pm on Saturday and closed on Sunday. The Master's House was extensively restored between 2011 and 2015 and

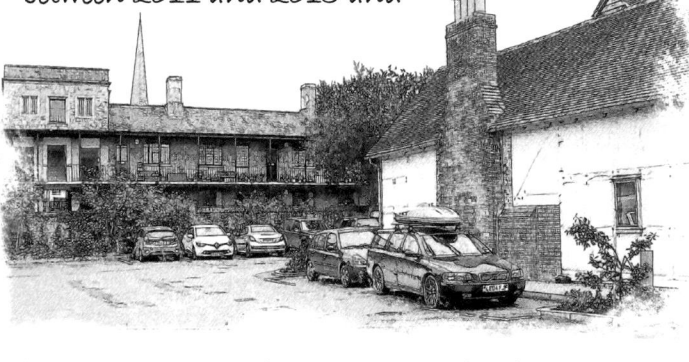

is now a community hub, a Public Library, a Community Services Centre providing registrar's services and ceremony space which are located in the impressive Great Hall and adjacent rooms.

On first entering the Great Hall it is easy to see that it was built to impress.

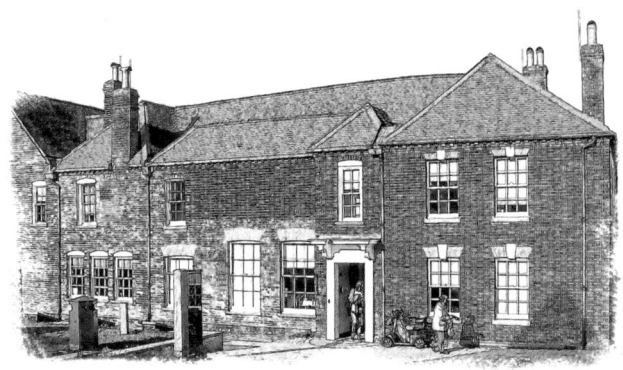

St. Katherine's Hospital was founded in 1232 by Bishop Hugo Foliot 'to the honour of the Lord and of St Katherine the Virgin'. It was built to provide for the spiritual as well as the material well-being of the poor, sick and to provide for travellers and the aged. The original hospital contained accommodation for the master and brethren and due to generous endowments a considerable estate has been acquired to support the operation of the hospital. The estate included an ale house, wash house, stable, cattle sheds, sheep pens and barn. By the 16th century the estate included a hostel in the form of Almshouses, a chapel and a substantial Master's House. However, the management and development of St. Katherine's was not always blessed with integrity. At the time the Black Death was sweeping through the country, Pope

John XXII had to write in 1322 to the Abbot of Wigmore instructing him to prevent the master from squandering the resources of the hospital with their fraudulent activities. A century later it is suggested that the corrupt masters had made substantial sums of money from the hospital estate and one master became wealthy enough to have a substantial house built away from the common dormitory which is the present day Masters House that was built in 1487.

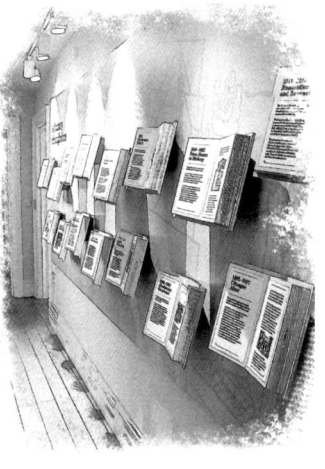

To better understand the development of The Masters House and St Katherine's Hospital from 1231 to present day, an interesting historical tour is made available through a Tablet with headphones which can be obtained free of charge from the reception counter. One of the Masters of St Katherine's, Edward Cowper has left the most detailed records and accounts between 1584 and 1595. This has allowed modern day archivists to understand the daily undertakings of the Master and his employees. The Tablet tour is based upon a number of the Master's House characters and their roles in providing a service to maintain the daily functions of the brethren.

In October 2013 a fascinating record of the 15th century interior was portrayed in the Malvern Gazette and Ledbury Reporter as the £2.9million restoration work was undertaken.

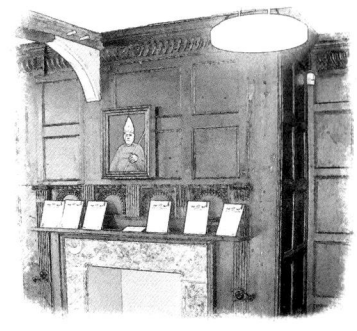

On leaving the Master's House the large map on the stone plinth provides a reference point to the

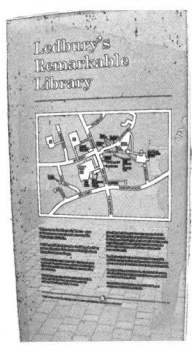

geography of the area. A layout of the original site has been created on the paving stones in front of the map. A little further on is a set of six sandstone display boards describing the characters that appear on the tablet tour.

Now head towards the High Street and walk past St Katherine's Hall and Chapel which are on the right. On entering the high street the delightful bustle of this ancient market town comes into its own with the iconic Market House opposite and the most spectacular display of black and white timbered buildings which could grace any high street.

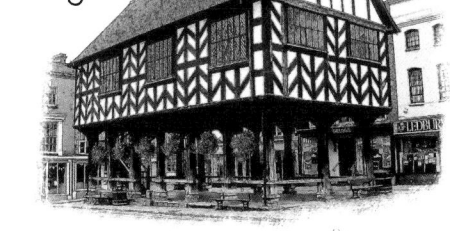

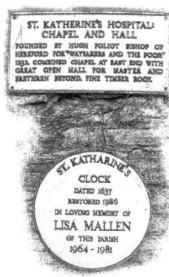

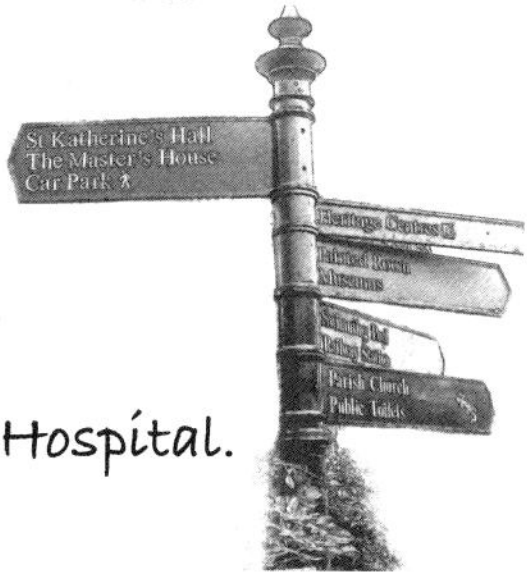

Immediately to the left are the almshouses of St. Katherine's Hospital.

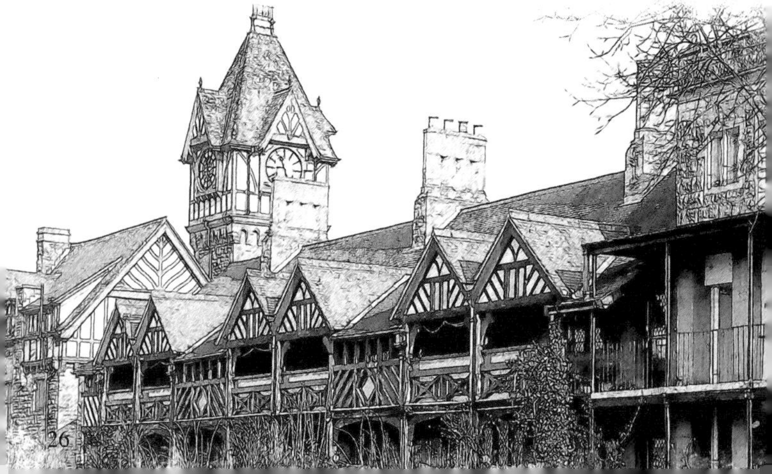

Keep left towards the bus stop and the stone cattle drinking trough which is planted with flowers
to the front of St. Katherine's. A stone plaque by the main gates of St. Katherine's describes how Robert Smirk was the designer when the almshouses were extended during Victorian Times.

> THE ALMSHOUSES
> ST KATHERINE'S HOSPITAL
> The south wing was built by Sir Robert Smirke in 1822.
> north wing, built in 1866, replaced earlier half-timbered houses
> when the Brethren abandoned communal life in the Chapel.

In 1822 all the original timber framed almshouses dating back to the 16th century were demolished and stone almshouses were built in their place with an additional row constructed a few years later in 1866. The stone memorial pays tribute to the dead of two world wars and is to the front on the gates.

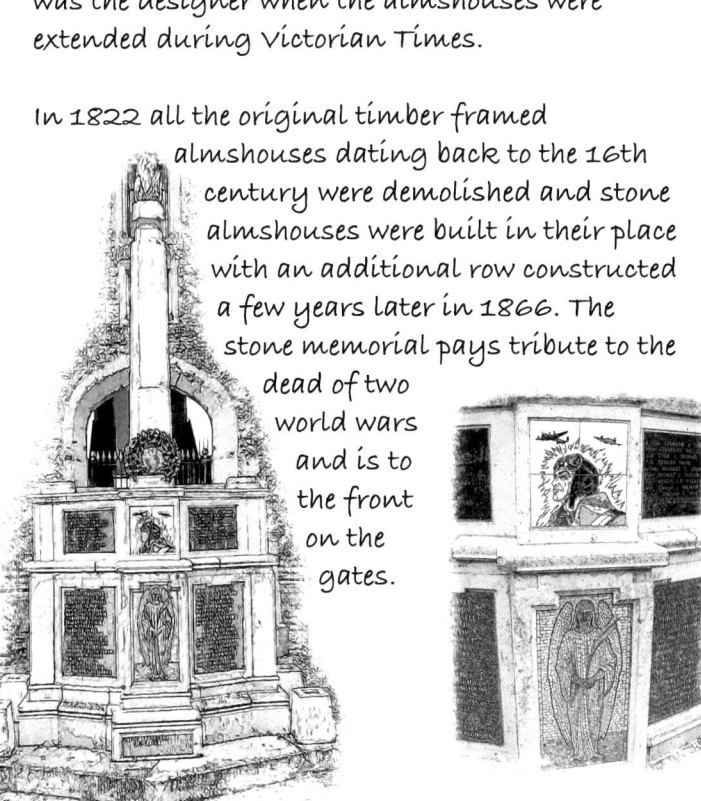

Looking across the road to the Market House it would not be amiss to wonder as to why the road is quite so wide. Originally in front of the almshouses was another row of buildings called Butchers Row. The history of this development is quite fascinating. Firstly, temporary market stalls were brought here on Market Days. But probably due to the width of the road there was no external pressure to remove the stalls. Over time they became established as permanent buildings. A number of these stalls were butchers premises and as was the custom in those days, animals were slaughtered and sold to feed the town and country folk particularly on market days. Not to put too fine a point on the description of such activities, the archives describe that there were loud squeals as the animals were killed and rivers of blood were in the gutters as the butchery took place. Fires were maintained to singe the hair off the slaughtered pigs. This was certainly not a welcome sight or aroma for the stage coach traveller on gaining their first impressions of Ledbury. This negative impact on the genteel development of the town was clearly identified by the influential John Biddulph and Thomas Baylis amongst others. Thus Butchers Row had to go. Petitions and public meetings were held to remove this eyesore, but compensation was needed to displace the proprietors of Butchers Row. This took a number of years with considerable expense.

It was not until 1840 that the fourteen butcher's stalls and five shambles were demolished. One of the buildings still survives and has been relocated to Church Lane and is now the Butchers Row Museum.

At the far end of the almshouse wall to the left is a plaque bearing the unusual title of the 'Cathol until 1835 site of alley between almshouses and Butchers Row'.

BARRETT BROWNING INSTITUTE
THE HOMEND
COMMEMORATES ELIZABETH BARRETT BROWNING, POETESS, WHO SPENT HER CHILDHOOD IN THE DISTRICT. BUILT ON SITE OF THE OLD TANNERY. OPENED BY SIR HENRY RIDER HAGGARD, 1896.

Cross over Bye Street towards the tall tower of the Victorian built Barrett Browning Memorial Institute. This originally contained a reading room, library and meeting rooms. The road from now on is named the Homend. This name was first recorded in 1288 and was derived from the Old English word 'hamm' or 'hom' which probably means 'land hemmed in by water or marsh' or 'river meadow'.

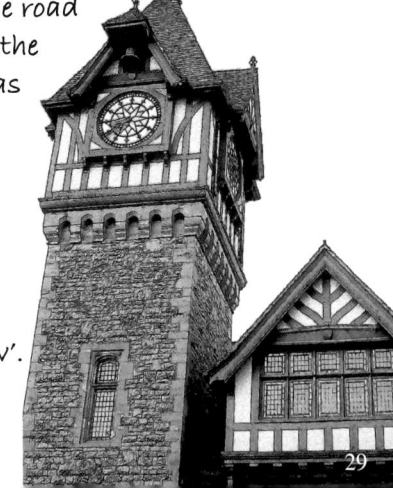

The first and probably the largest of the alleyways to be encountered on this walk is 'Skipp Alley' which is just past the NatWest Bank.

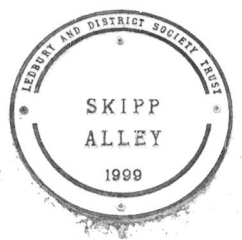

Very shortly after is 'Scattergood's yard'.

Take a look through the wrought iron gate at this pretty passageway. A little further on 'Ice Bytes' cyber cafe contains what is left of the Tourist Information Centre. A few paces further on is the attractive black and white timbered Olive Tree Italian restaurant.

After window shopping the extensive menu of the Olive Tree, next door is the very popular Homend Bakery Shop.

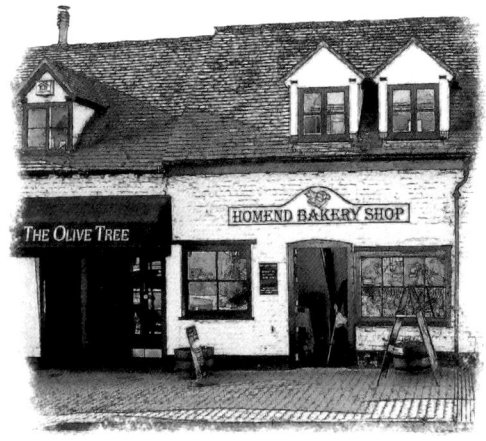

A few doors further on, in the style of many fish and chips shops across the country, is the appropriately named 'The Codfather Part II'.

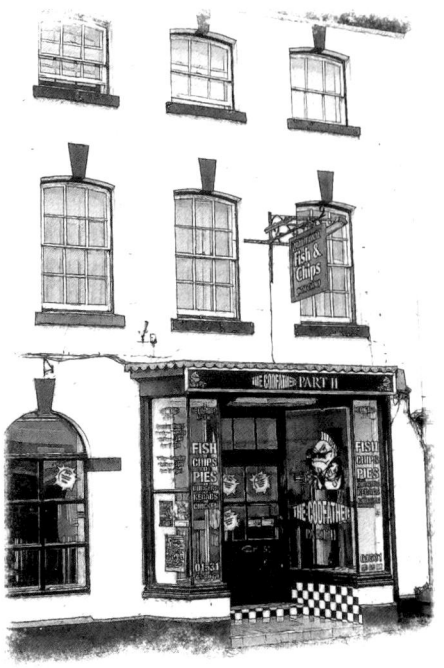

Continuing with the walk, 'Hodges Yard' at 262 the Homend is a delightful black and white timbered yard to explore.

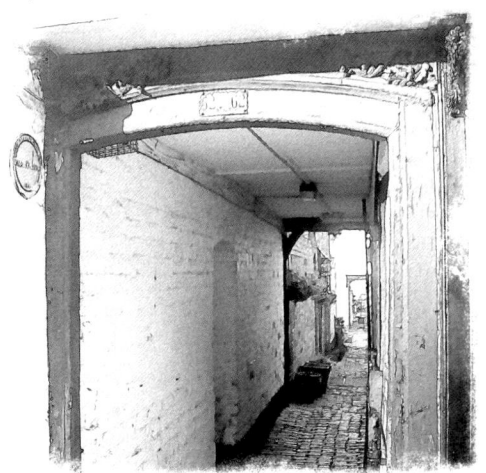

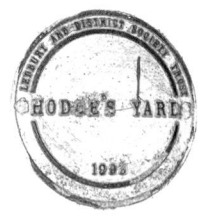

There is also 'The Hodges' monument in the Ledbury Parish churchyard. The narrow 'Fox Lane led to Hills Yard' according to the cast iron plaque and goes left between the buildings and onto more modern developments.

Next is the three storey former Plough Hotel indicated by the wooden gates into Plough Yard.

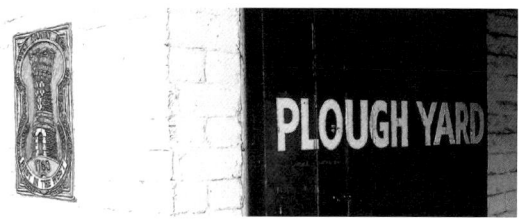

In September 1914 there was a mysterious death here. Four men from the Birmingham area were hop picking in nearby Bosbury and came into Ledbury. After eating and drinking at a couple of establishments they stopped here for a quart of ale between them. One of them had found half a mug of beer on the counter and emptied it into their jug. A little later on all four were found pretty near unconscious. Two policemen and a doctor attempted to revive them but Harry Ansell died. According to the Ledbury Guardian the doctor who carried out the post mortem said that "his air passages contained a certain amount of green material. Both his lungs were seriously diseased, and of long standing. His heart was fatty, and the stomach contained the same green material." But what was the cause of death? No one could account for what was contained in the half-full mug, nor had the Landlord or serving girl seen the mug on the counter. All very strange!

It is probably best at this point in the walk to describe why Ledbury has so many alleyways of which there are some 23 in this walk. During the middle ages the development of Ledbury was planned by the Bishop of Hereford, the High Street and Homend was divided into narrow strips just 22 feet wide but stretching back from this tiny frontage some 200 feet or more. These were known as burgage plots. The burgage was a plot of land to which was attached specific liabilities and privileges. This thin strip of land allowed trade and workshop premises to have a frontage with accommodation above and to the rear with space for livestock, storage and vegetable gardens. The plague years (1349, 1360 and 1370) saw many properties become vacant and therefore a number of these thin burgage plots were amalgamated to form more substantial frontages such as seen with the Feathers Hotel, The Talbot and Ledbury Park. However, with the less affluent owners, many of the Burgage plots were sub-divided into half, quarters and even eighths. The issue of gaining access to the rear of the Burgage and these sub-divisions was achieved through the development of side alleys.

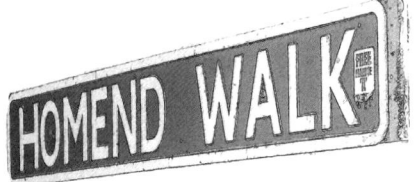

Next the tiny Homend Walk leads to a couple of retailers and this is followed by the next alleyway 'Thorne's Place' which was formerly Madders Yard.

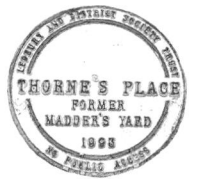

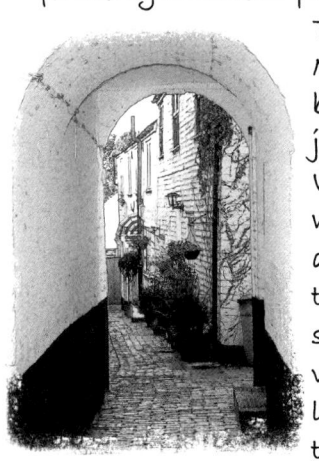

The name Madders can just be seen painted on the bricks just beneath the roof line. William Madders and Son were grocers and hardware dealers. A picture from the 'Old Ledbury' website shows that the building was virtually demolished when a lorry crashed into the front of the shop.

Continue away from Ledbury town centre and cross the road named Belle Orchard which leads to modern terrace houses. As the Baptist Church is passed the Esso Garage comes into view in the distance with on the left the last alleyway on this side of the Homend, the White Horse former Inn and yard.

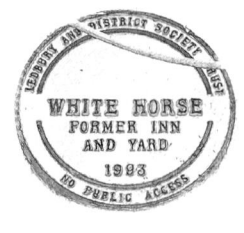

It is probably best to cross over to the other side of the Homend via the traffic lights at the entrance to the Tesco supermarket. However, before you cross over, look over the road at the early 17th century cruck truss on the house opposite. This building technique goes back to pre-Norman and most probably Celtic times. The cruck frame consists of a pair of curved timbers known as the cruck blades, which were often cut from one tree. A tie-beam or collar helps to join the blades together. With a careful look you will see to the right of the end wall window a section of wood which appears to be missing. It is not in fact, but some years ago there was a chimney here which had to be demolished and the wall was re-rendered covering up the timbers.

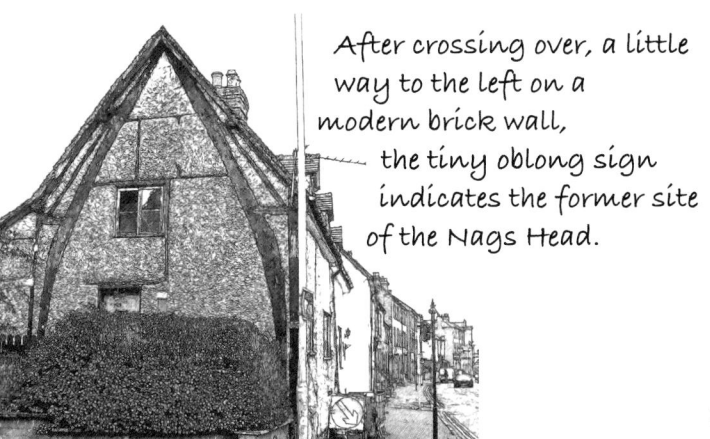

After crossing over, a little way to the left on a modern brick wall, the tiny oblong sign indicates the former site of the Nags Head.

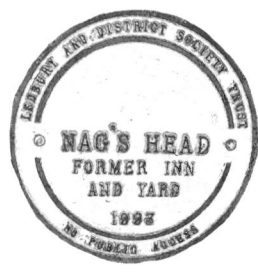

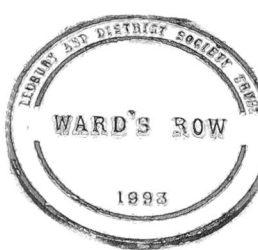

Looking towards the Esso garage but on the opposite side of the road is a large Victorian House obscured by trees. This is where the budding Poet Laureate John Masefield lived. It was named the Knapp and was built by his father Edward Masefield. It is hardly worth visiting the house as it is surrounded by a large wall and hidden from view behind substantial shrubs and trees.

This is where we turn back towards the town.

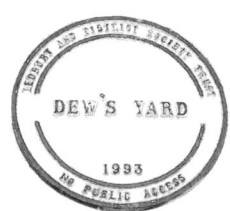

A small brick alleyway is indicated by the Wards Row plaque. A few doors further on above a doorway is the plaque for Dews Yard.

Number 153 The Homend looks like it should be a yard as the Methodist Church

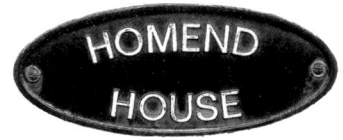

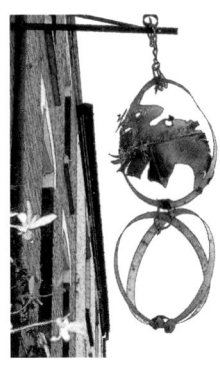

comes into view. The houses in this section of the Homend are quite substantial, with two fine examples, Homend House resplendent with a hanging leaf sculpture and opposite Melrose House.

As the slight corner is turned, the Barrett Browning Memorial Institute comes back into view.

Bill's Yard is next on the left and then the plaque for the Common Garden alley which is hidden under the awning for Isaacs Linen shop.

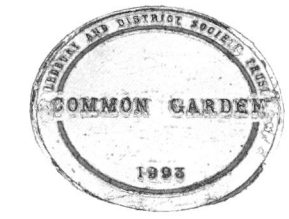

The alleyway looks well used and heads uphill. Continuing into town, the colourfully attired complete with delivery bicycle stationed above the shop front of DT Waller and Sons is one of Ledbury's premier butchers.

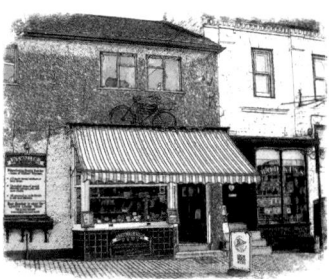

Tucked away next door is Smoke Alley which was originally called Smock Alley.

The 1851 census indicated that 61 people lived in 13 houses down this alley. The little plaque indicates the original house numbers 43-65 in the alleyway.

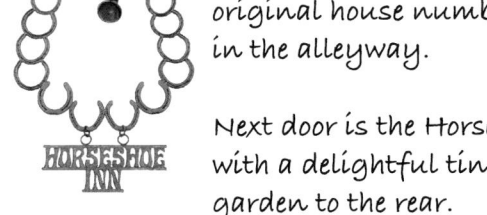

Next door is the Horseshoe Inn with a delightful tiny beer garden to the rear.

Cross over Bank Crescent to Jenkins the fresh fruit and vegetable shop. A little further on is Ledbury's next amazing butcher, the Llandinabo farm shop. Since 2005 it has been run as the flagship store of the Traditional Breeds Meat Marketing Company. The butcher only sells meat from pedigree, rare and traditional breeds. A little further on the Velvet Bean chocolate shop is a chocoholics delight as the most wonderful aroma of warm chocolate invites you to enter this tiny emporium.

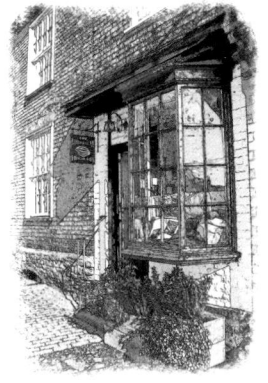

A little further on there is an unmarked pretty black and white timbered alley just before the Seven Stars pub.

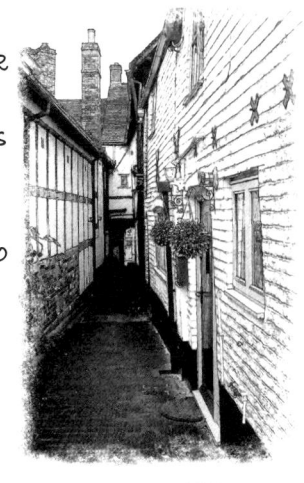

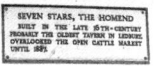

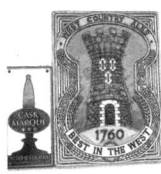

The Homend Mews has two picturesque entrances and is located behind the sweet shop.

The Muse cafe provides a pleasant courtyard dining experience. Note the mouse hole by the step.

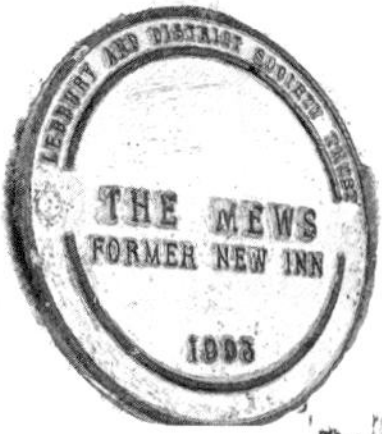

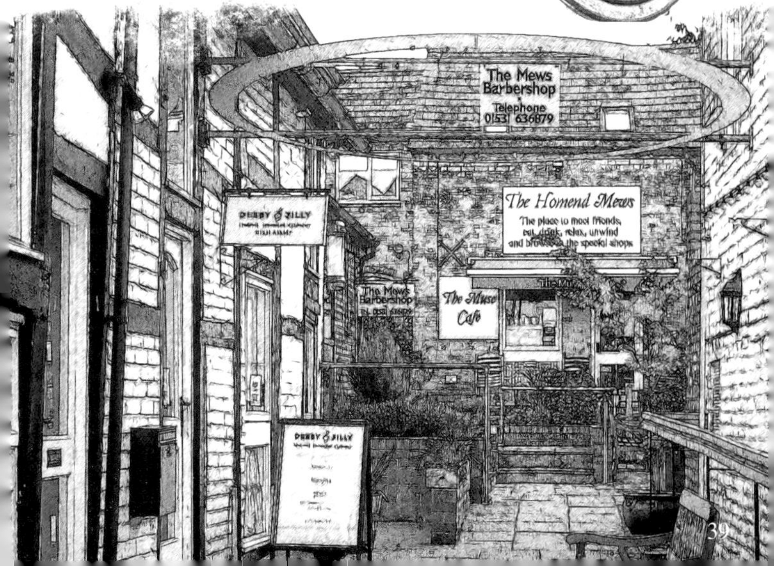

On exiting continue past or indeed go into the Three Counties Cider Shop. The range of ciders produced in the Three Counties is quite considerable.

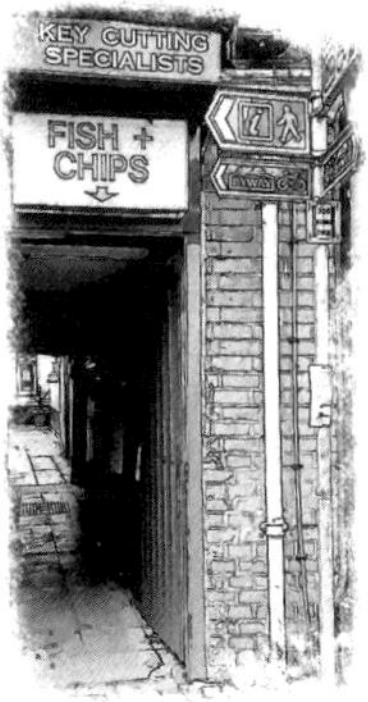

The next alley I have named fish and chip alley as there is no plaque but an inviting sign to enjoy take-away fish and chips. On reaching the corner next to the impressive market house, turn left past the Market House Cafe and Delicatessen into the attractively cobbled Church Walk.

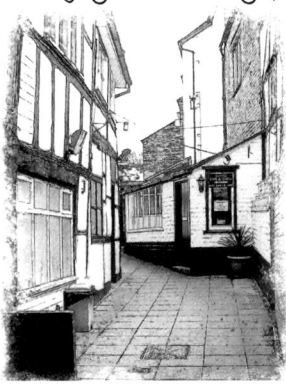

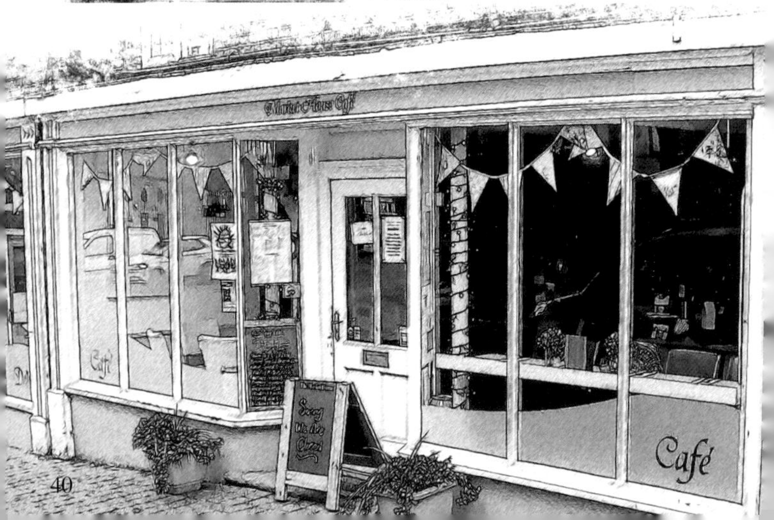

At the entrance there is normally an array of hoardings advertising the eateries to be found close by.

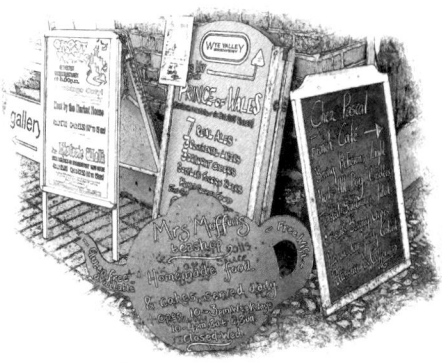

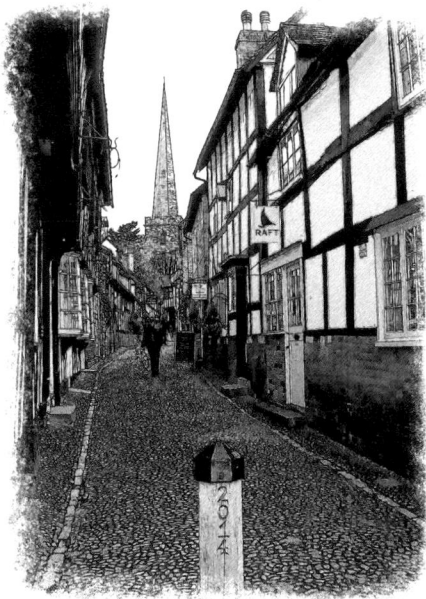

Looking up the left-hand side of the lane the first attractive black and white timbered building dates back to early Tudor times and houses the Town Council Offices.

OLD COUNCIL OFFICES,
CHURCH STREET
BUILT ABOUT 1500, VARIOUSLY USED AS POOR LAW INSTITUTION, FIRST TOWN LIBRARY AND COUNCIL OFFICES.

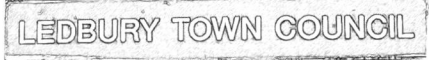

Purely by chance during internal renovation a wonderful array of 16th century wall paintings were discovered. The paintings are based on designs and inscriptions, imitating expensive tapestries and wall hangings found in higher status Elizabethan homes. The 16th century Painted Room is open to the public and guides provide a short talk. Due to the frailty of the wall paintings the moisture content of the air is monitored by limiting the group size. Admission is free.

A little further on, the public toilets have been cleverly blended into the architecture of the lane.

Then follows the exceptional Prince of Wales public house which dates from the 15th or 16th century. It serves up a range of excellent real ales, cider and tasty food, particularly the faggots which are so popular in Ledbury.

Further on is the Museum and Heritage Centre which is believed to have been built circa 1500 for an East Anglian wool merchant.

An interesting feature is that a stream ran under the building and was probably used for washing the wool fleeces. The stream bed can be seen through a glass panel constructed into the floor. Later in the 16th century, the building was converted to a grammar school. In 1799, the last master of the school, Mr William Humphreys was appointed by the Bishop of Hereford. He maintained the school into his old age but with dwindling pupil numbers the school closed around 1830. It then was divided up into five tenements until 1969. Following years of neglect it has been restored to its present day splendour.

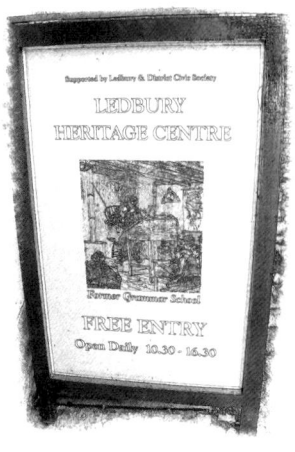

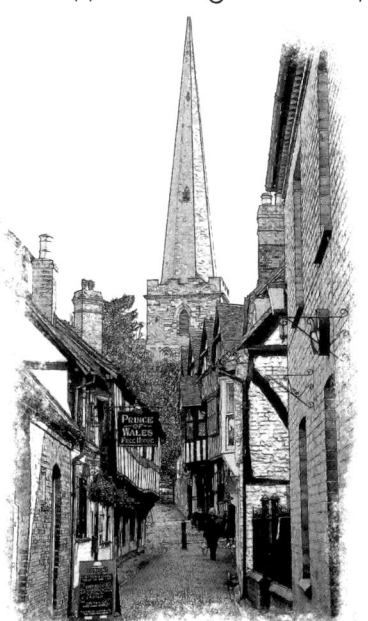

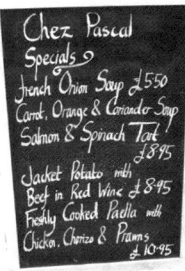

Looking up the right hand side of the lane there is the 'Raft' clothes shop then Mrs Muffins Teashop, then follows Chez Pascal, a family run French Brasserie.

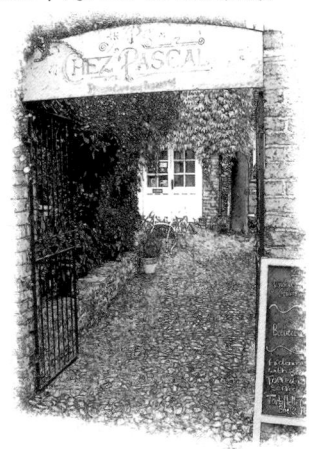

Further on the Butchers Row House Museum is set back a little from the lane, behind a pretty courtyard.

The present day museum was originally one of the Butchers Row buildings mentioned previously.

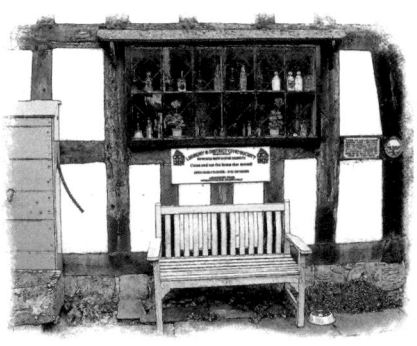

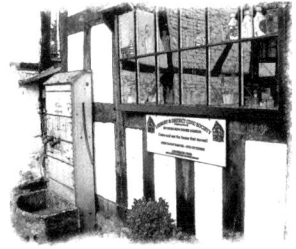

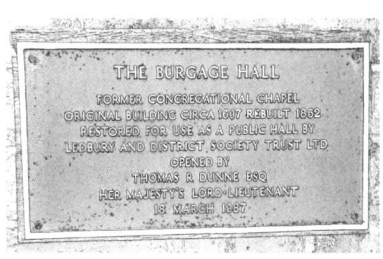

Behind the museum is the Burgage Hall which was built in 1852. It was originally built as a meeting house for the Congregational Chapel.

Spend some time taking in all that this wonderful lane has to offer.

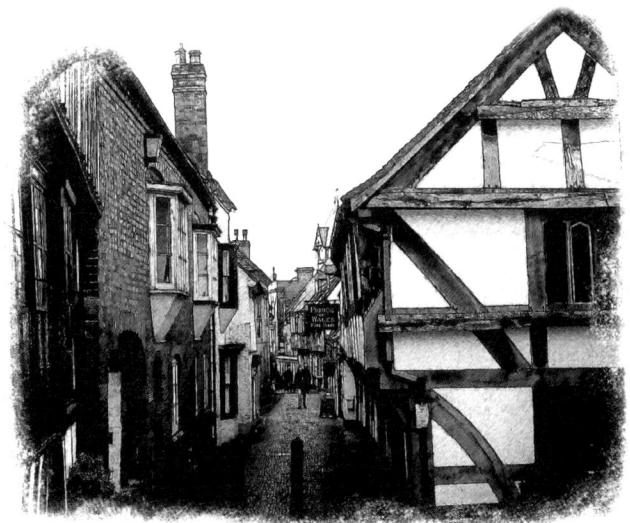

On approaching the end of the lane on the right there is a black and white timbered building named the Tannery.

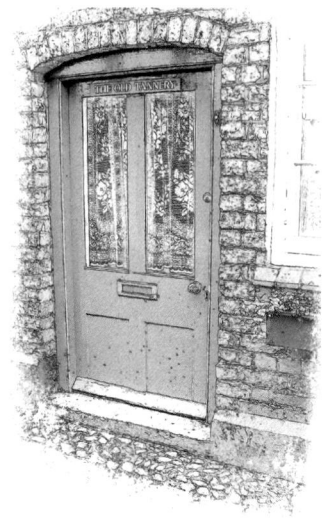

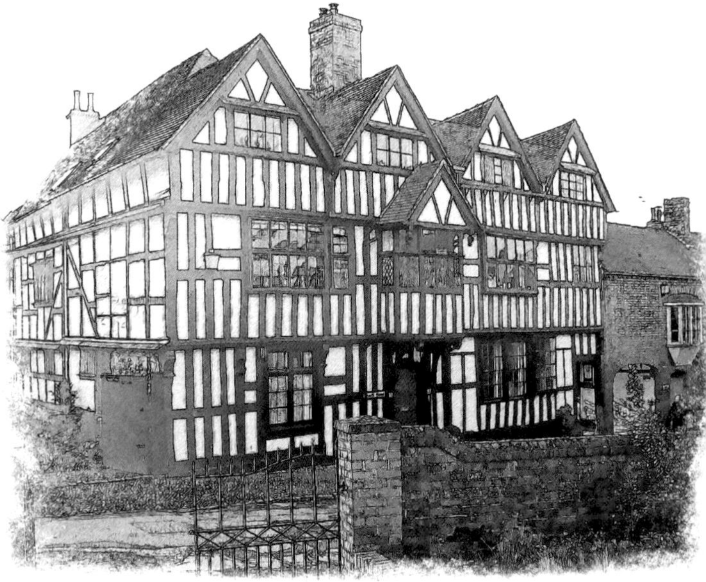

Next is a courtyard entrance and then the 16th century Church House where posters indicate that the John Masefield Poetry Society is located here.

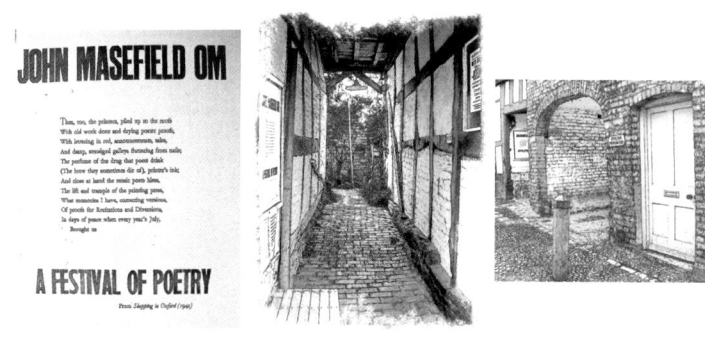

At the top of the lane, set back from the lane is the earlier 15th century Abbot's Lodge which was once the vicarage.

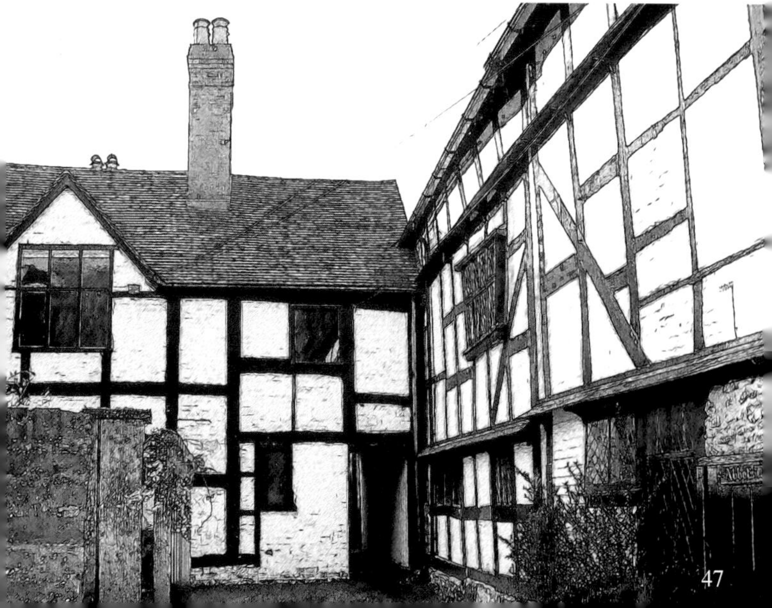

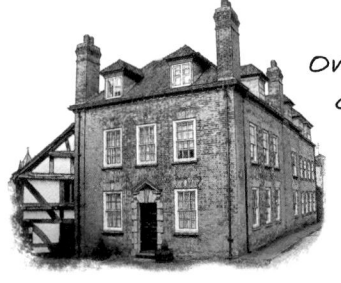

On the left the impressive Georgian styled Old Magistrates House stands proud. It was a police station with the Magistrates' Court and cells behind. Look opposite towards the delightful Walled Garden and the entrance to the churchyard at grid reference SO 71263 37687.

Ledbury Parish Church of St Michael and All Angels was described by Nikolaus Pevsner as 'the premier parish church of Herefordshire'. In 1086 The Domesday Book identifies a Minster Church. By 1140 the church had been rebuilt and had become a Portionist church with two dignitaries of Hereford Cathedral known as Portionists being granted residence near the church. They had the right to appropriate revenue and appoint a vicar.

The first mention of the name of a vicar was John de Almeley in 1300.

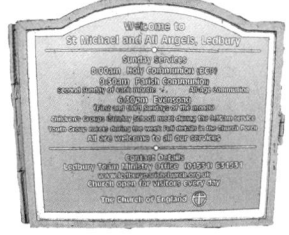

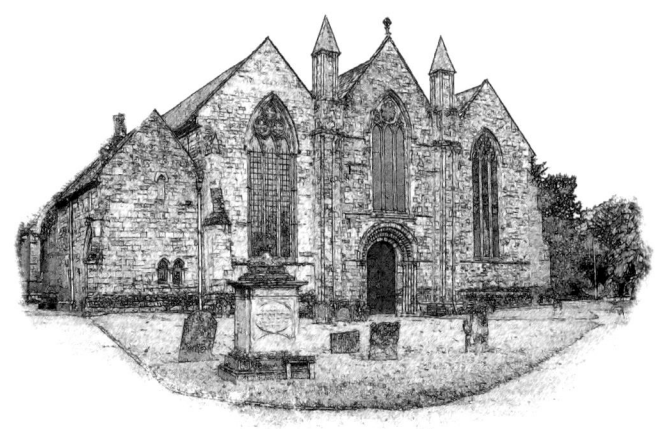

The church has unusually a separate bell tower containing eight bells with the oldest dating from 1690. The tower was constructed in four stages, the three lower ones date from about 1230 and the fourth taking the height to 202ft is the spire which was built in 1733. Although detached belfries are uncommon in the UK there are a further six in Herefordshire.

The church clock activates a carillon which plays a repertoire of seven hymn tunes at three-hourly intervals during the day from 9am, 12 noon, 3pm and 6pm. To hear the Carillon scan the QR Code.

The main entrance is on the north side of the church, through the double doors. The second set of doors looks quite rough and marked. This is the damage caused by musket fire during the English Civil War. Take a few moments to look for a number of musket balls still embedded in the wood. The first impression on entering the church is its sheer size.

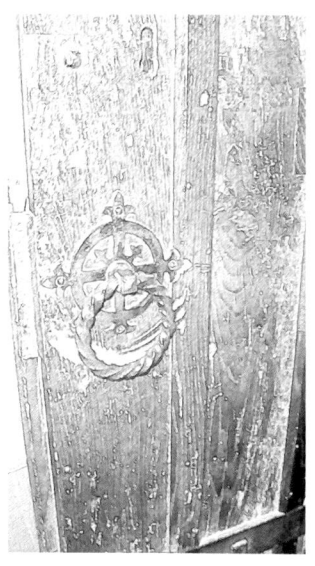

To begin a brief tour of the church, keep to the right along the west wall. The impressive centre aisle leads the eye to the painting of the 'Last Supper'. This is a copy of Leonardo de Vinci's work which was painted by local artist, Thomas Ballard in 1824.

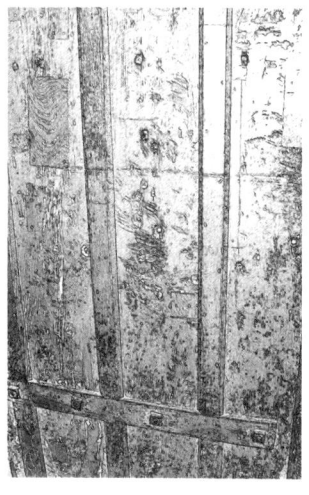

In the far south west corner is the imposing Biddulph family vault.

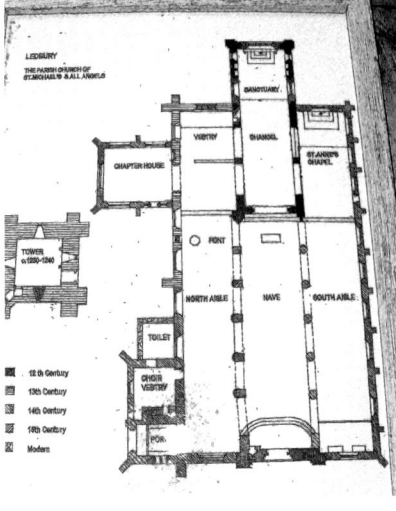

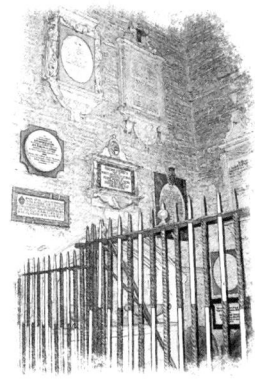

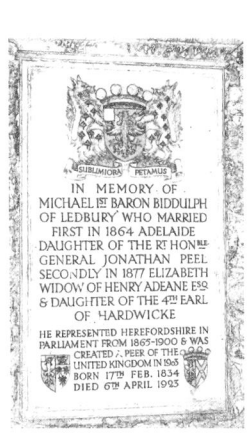

IN MEMORY OF
MICHAEL 1ST BARON BIDDULPH
OF LEDBURY WHO MARRIED
FIRST IN 1864 ADELAIDE
DAUGHTER OF THE RT HON BLE
GENERAL JONATHAN PEEL
SECONDLY IN 1877 ELIZABETH
WIDOW OF HENRY ADEANE ESQ
& DAUGHTER OF THE 4TH EARL
OF HARDWICKE

HE REPRESENTED HEREFORDSHIRE IN
PARLIAMENT FROM 1865-1900 & WAS
CREATED A PEER OF THE
UNITED KINGDOM IN 1903
BORN 17TH FEB. 1834
DIED 6TH APRIL 1923

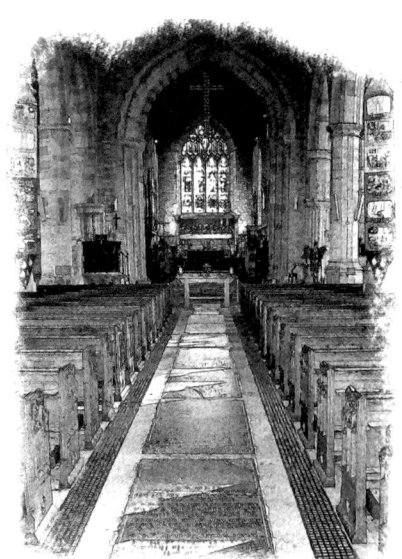

Continuing along the south wall there is a memorial to Captain Skinner. Further along there are an interesting collection of bibles going back to 1610 and prayer books from 1659.

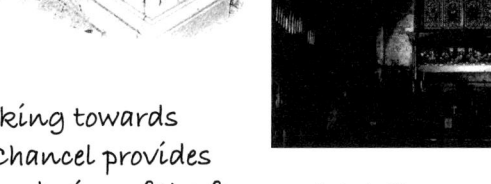

The St Anne's Chapel is located in the southern corner. On the east wall look for the memorial to the Moulton Barrett's, parents of Elizabeth Barrett Browning.

Walking towards the Chancel provides a superb view of the famous Last Supper oil painting.

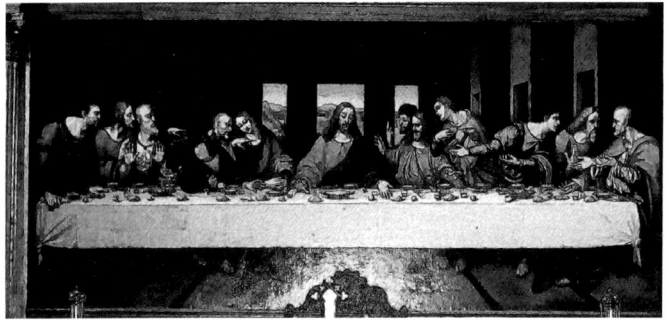

On the right the intricately carved Skynner family tomb is resplendent.

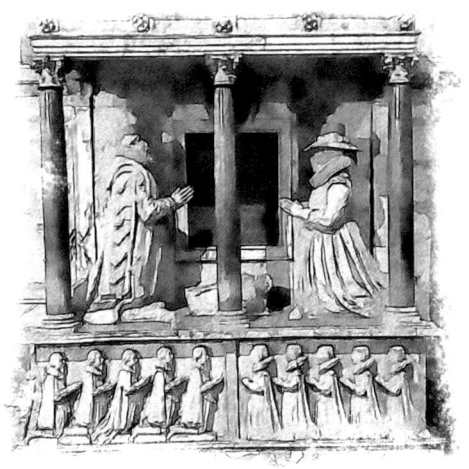

Many of the guide books and websites refer to Elizabeth Skynner's Jacobean-style hat and her Elizabethan-style dress and ruff. Notice the child reclining at the back and the first of the kneeling daughters both clasping a skull (Do note that the skull held by the kneeling daughter is now missing) this is an indication that they predeceased their parents.

Above the tomb on the south wall there is an uncommon facet in the design of the modern stained glass church

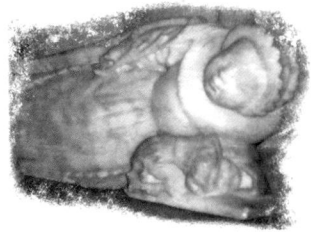

window where snow is depicted in the scenery of St Martin of Tours cutting his cloak in half to give to a beggar.

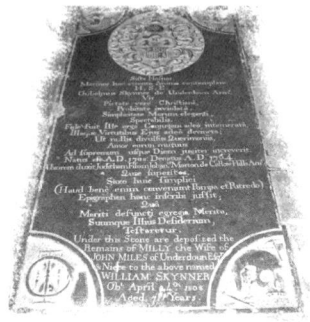 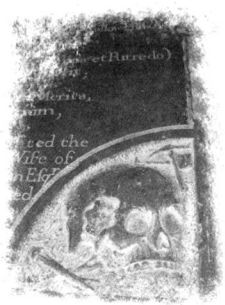

Over to the north side of the church on the stone floor are some interesting tomb stones including the Skynners. The small metal plaque on the wall describes:

'Here lyeth the body of Theo Cupper of Climpton Oxfordshire esquire who being of age 70 years was made immortal 27th of June 1621. Dead yes and wormed admit he be what then he lives inclosed in the hearts of men'.

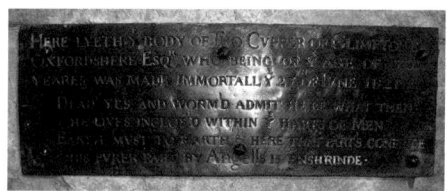

Interesting to observe that some of the Old English spellings have been corrected on the plaque.

The hole in the wall or squint into the North Chapel allowed those parishioners who were suffering from skin disease (this was generally called Leprosy but was a catchall for all skin ailments) to see

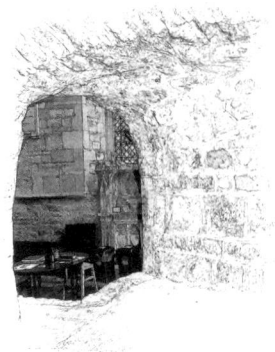

the vicar leading the service without themselves being seen by the congregation in days gone by.

Continuing past the North Chapel is the Chapter House which was built in 1330. This was an extension to the church and is now used for parish meetings. The North aisle returns to the North Door via a copy of Botticelli's Madonna and Child and another lesser valued painting of the Last Supper.

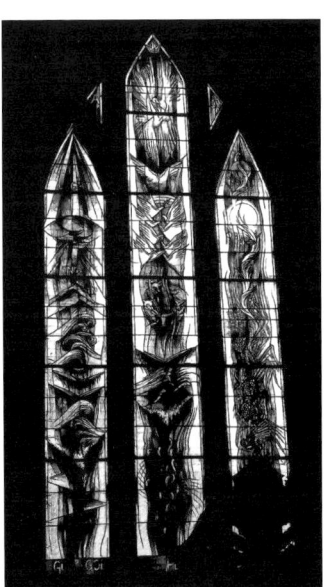

On exiting the church opposite the north door look for the rare style of triangular box tomb.

The cemetery is a little unusual in that it is mainly situated on the north side of the church. The most likely reason for this is that the stream which you can see redirected at the far end of the churchyard, enclosed by metal railings used to flow down the south side of the churchyard and along Church Lane. It is very likely that this is the stream that flowed under the Heritage Centre and across to Bye Street where the unsightly and very smelly waste from Butchers Row would be washed away.

Walk around the church to the left. Along the south wall of the church are a number of wooden benches. The first has a small square QR code attached and if scanned by a mobile phone a poem can be heard from the 'Bench Poems Project'

undertaken by Ledbury Primary School during the Ledbury Poetry Festival. Opposite the bench in the churchyard, a signpost indicates the Garden of Remembrance.

The Blacksmith's Tomb is quite well known. It is the tomb of Thomas Russell which is said to have inspired John Masefield's poem Blacksmith's Epitaph. The witty epitaph reads:

'My sledge and hammer lie reclined, My bellows too have lost their wind. My fire's extinct, my forge decayed, and in the dust my vice is laid. My coal is spent, my iron gone. My firedried corpse now lies at rest. My soul smoke-like is soaring to be blest'

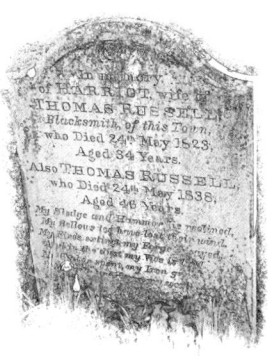

The final two lines are missing due to weather damage to the gravestone. Further research has indicated that the same inscription can be found on the gravestone for George Jones, village blacksmith', in Old Cleve Churchyard, Somerset.

After enjoying the inscription follow the path round to the right, heading away from the entrance to

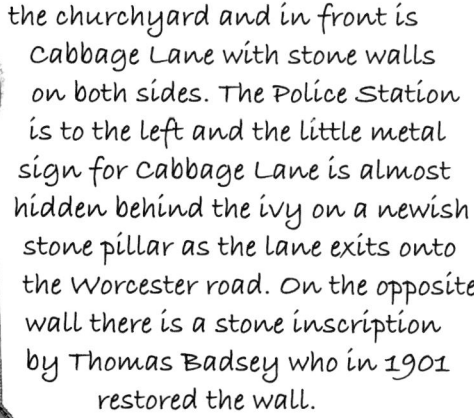

the churchyard and in front is Cabbage Lane with stone walls on both sides. The Police Station is to the left and the little metal sign for Cabbage Lane is almost hidden behind the ivy on a newish stone pillar as the lane exits onto the Worcester road. On the opposite wall there is a stone inscription by Thomas Badsey who in 1901 restored the wall.

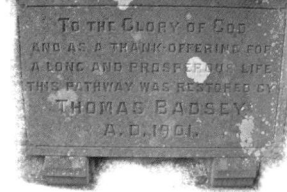

Walk past Masefield Solicitors, the same family as the poet Laureate John Masefield. Opposite are the new buildings and gates into Ledbury Park.

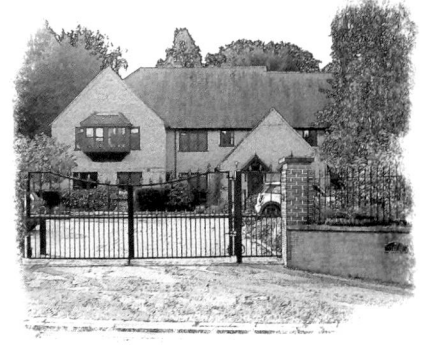

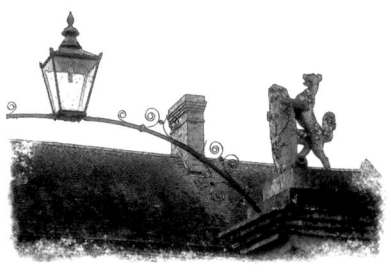

On the right hand side set back from the road is the impressive looking Priory Lodge and Priory Gatehouse.

The Ledbury Guide of 1824 describes this as

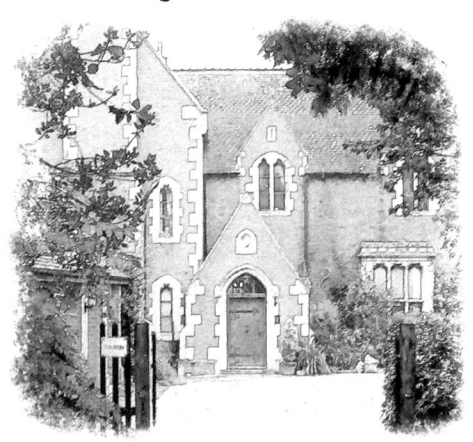

'Mr Dunn's Academy'. Hidden away behind the first house on the Worcester Road and the gravel driveway to Priory Lodge is the secluded Public Footpath into Tilley's Alley.

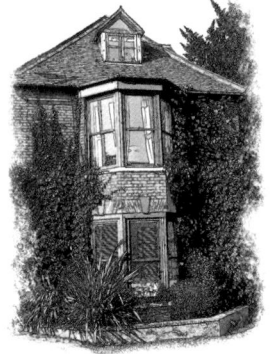

This is a delightful courtyard and was in 1530 the site of the King's Arms Inn which had its frontage on the High Street. It closed in 1778.

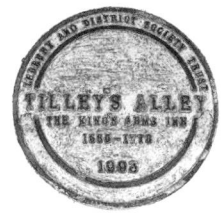

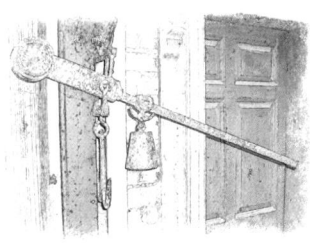

The yard is named after the successful business orientated Tilley family who owned motor accessory, car and cycle hire premises, bookshop, stationers and to this day 'Tilley Printing' which was established as a letterpress in 1875.

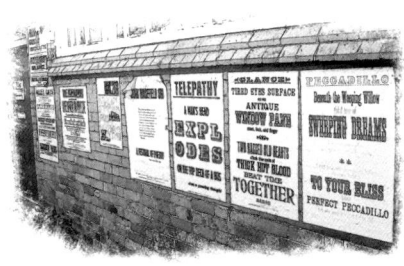

There is a colourful display of their printed posters on the wall of the press. The narrow alleyway leads out into the busy High Street.

Turn right passing four shop fronts turn right again into the

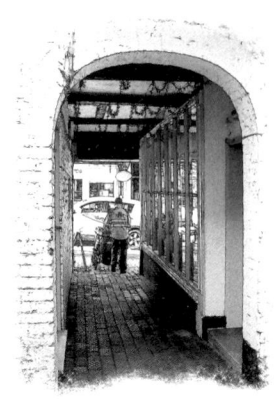

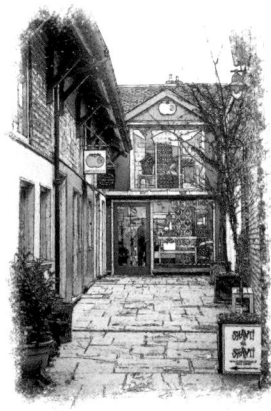

Design Quarter alleyway next door to the excellent Gurneys the butchers at number 12 The High Street. This has been a butcher's shop since 1871. This alley is a gem of old and contemporary design. The Hus Hem Scandinavian design shop, Shanti-Shanti

handicrafts and Serenity hairdressers provide a stunning reflection of sensitive design in a historical setting.

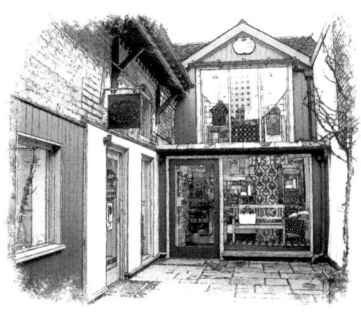

Turning right on exiting the alley is Ledbury's premier wine emporium, Hay Wines. Continue

past a few stores and into Tinsmith Alley this is alongside the most centrally located hostelry in Ledbury the Retreat Pub. The alley is colourfully decorated and the Tinsmith linens, fabrics and homeware shop is located in an extraordinary designed building. Both the Design Quarter and Tinsmiths Alley are worth visiting just from a design and architectural viewpoint.

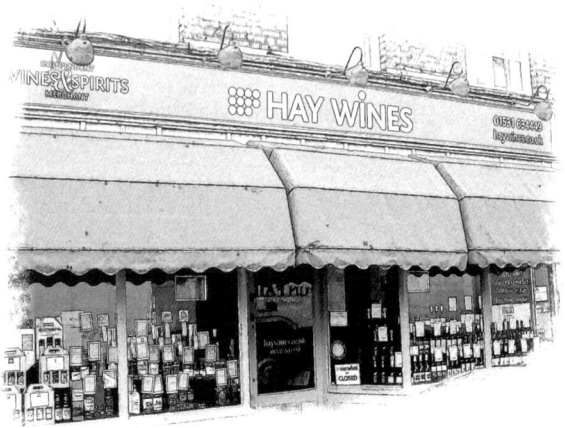

Tannery Lane is sometimes hidden by a door to the left of The Retreat Pub.

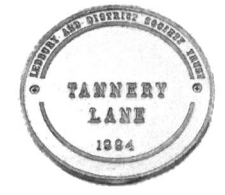

Continuing towards the Market House the last alley on this walk is Chapel alley, which as its name indicates leads to a Congregational Chapel which was founded in 1607 but closed in 1970.

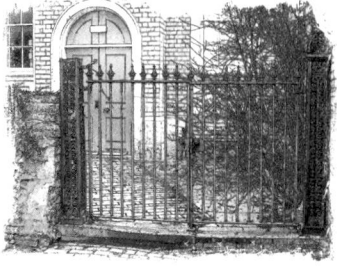

On returning to the high street spend some time looking at the iconic Market House. It was constructed in 1617 and altered after the English Civil War. The upper floor was originally used as a storeroom for grain, wool and hops when they were brought to market. It stands on sixteen oak pillars cut from the Malvern Forest. The open ground floor is used to this day as a market and information place. In the recent past the first floor was the Town Hall then it became a small theatre and was used for public meetings.

Turn back towards the pedestrian crossing and the St. Katherine's almshouses. Once over the road there is an opportunity for a further short excursion to complete the town centre heritage walk.

If time is available head up the High Street towards the Feathers Hotel. The Feathers Inn dates from 1560, and was originally two houses. During the plague years the burgage plots were amalgamated to form the current imposing site. It was an important coaching inn providing overnight accommodation for the Cheltenham to Aberystwyth stagecoach.

On approaching the cross-roads three sides of the junction are adorned with the most splendid black and white timbered buildings, the just mentioned Feathers Hotel, opposite the House on stilts and across the road is the impressive black

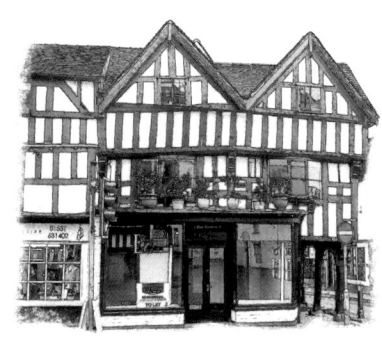

and white Ledbury Park House built by Edward Skinner, circa 1595.

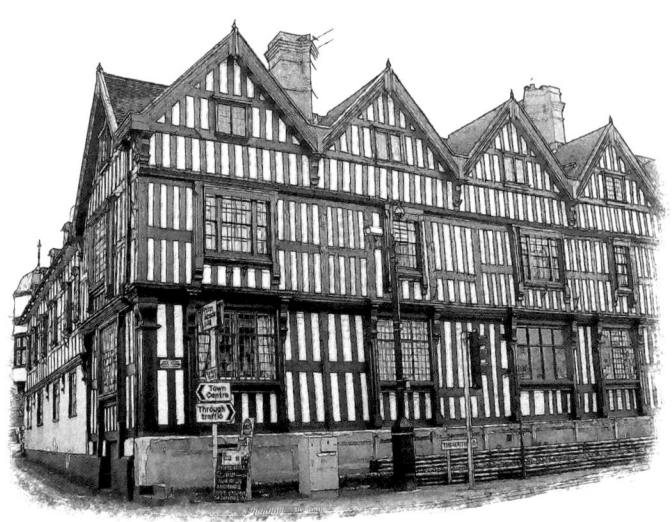

Originally it was named New House. Pevsner in 1963 described it as 'the grandest black and white house in the county'. The archives tell us that it was Prince Rupert's headquarters during the battle of Ledbury in 1645.

New Street was named a long time ago in 1232, surely by now it should be called 'Old Street'? Turn right into New Street and further down on

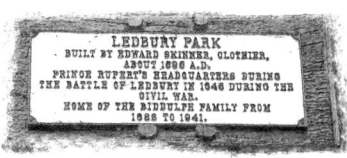

the left is the fine 16th century former coaching inn, the Talbot. Once inside the oak panelled dining room is impressive and the real ale very welcome after a walk.

After enjoying the pleasant atmosphere of this hostelry cross over the road and back towards the cross-roads. On the left is the rear entrance to the Feathers Hotel. The last time I walked through this entrance and car park an ancient Bugatti was being tended to by the AA man. The bar of the Feathers is very welcoming, modern and stylish and unsurprisingly serves great real ales and ciders.

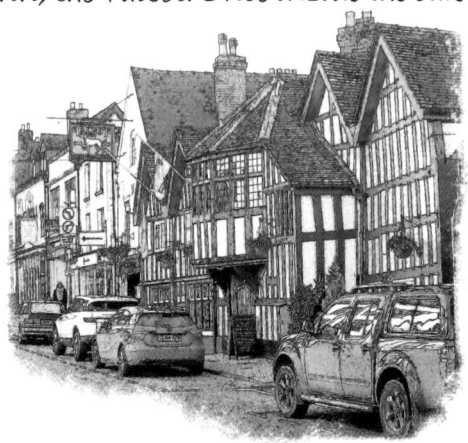

Notes and observations from the walk

Chapter 3

Walk 2

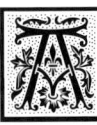round Ledbury Town: a brief history of transport in Ledbury

Summary
This circular walk features a disused canal, a dismantled railway, a current railway station, stunning town views and the old drovers route to Malvern and Worcester. The walk will take approximately one hour without stops. Walking boots are not necessary. It is buggy friendly except the climb over the only stile on the walk near Ledbury Railway station. Only one stile and one swing gate to navigate through.

Refreshment opportunities are numerous and are centred around the town sections of this walk.

Wells, springs and spouts
None

Places and points of interest
Masters House, Almshouses, Market Hall, Skew Bridge, Ledbury Railway Station, Dog Hill Wood, The Walled Garden and the Old Magistrates House.

Height map

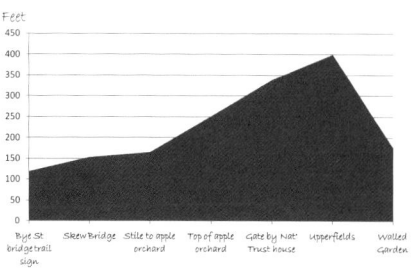

Connections to other walks
Walk 1 The Ledbury Town Centre Heritage Walk

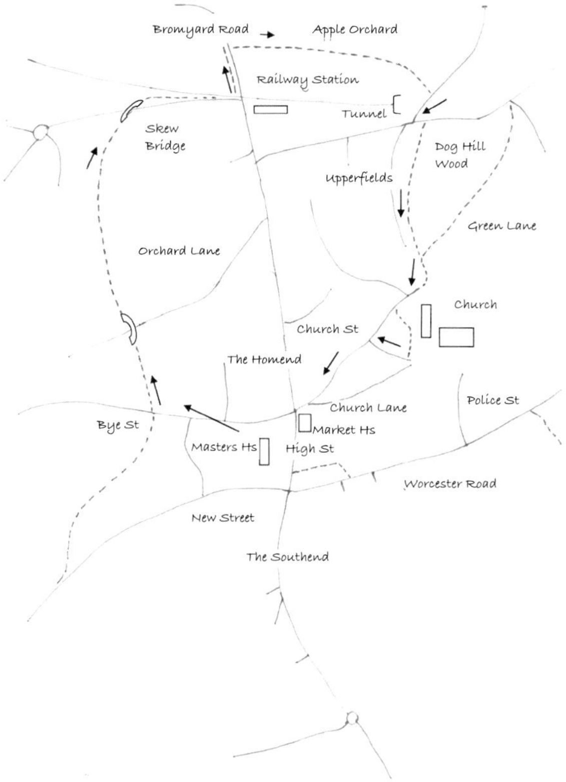

The Walk

This walk starts in Bye Street just a stone's throw from the town centre. So if arriving by car it is probably best to park in St Katherine's car park which is the main town centre pay and display car park next to St Katherine's Hospital and the Master's House.

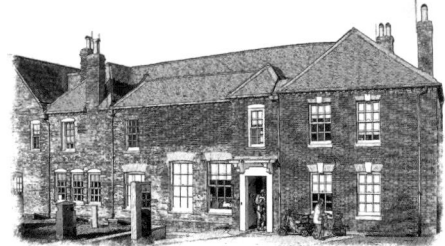

If arriving by train fast forward to the paragraph beginning 'There is an opportunity to visit the station....'. Walk towards Bye Street by heading out of the car park with the almshouses to the right and

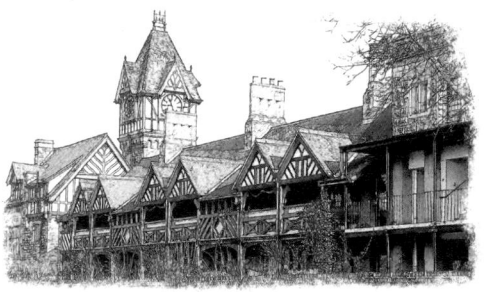

the Masters House to the left. As you turn to the left bearing away from the town centre the building opposite has a first floor loading bay which was built during the 19th century.

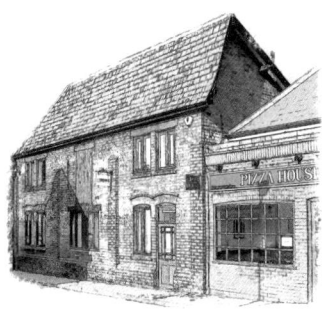

This was a string factory that supplied the hop industry until the 1960's. During the 17th century the original building here was a tannery. The unremarkable building to the immediate left was once a late medieval merchant's house.

As with the string factory the building has been substantially redeveloped over the centuries. A little way down on the right is the Fire Station and on the left is an unassuming cake shop called the Bakers Dozen. It is well worth visiting as they provide an interesting range of traditional pastries. Looking down the road, notice the row of four houses and then the fish and chip shop and Curry House appear to be in the middle of the original road.

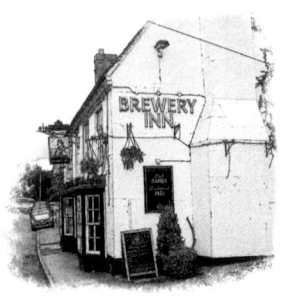

The Brewery Inn is tucked in behind this row of houses and shops. It was in earlier times known as the Boat which gives the first clue to the local history of this area of Ledbury. Both the pub and these dwellings would have played an important role in supporting the activities associated with the canal.

Walking past the Brewery Inn then leads onto a small grassy area where the Ledbury Town Trail information board is situated at map reference SO 70828 37690.

This is known as Queen's Walk. The grassed over space was formerly Ledbury Town Wharf where canal boats plied their trade between Hereford and Ledbury and the tidal reaches of the River Severn at Gloucester. When this was redeveloped for the railway it was known as Ledbury Halt.

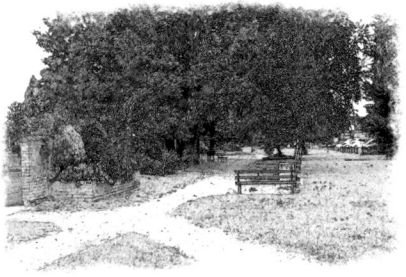

It is also recorded that Alfred Watkins who was famous

for his exposition on Lay Lines stopped here for the evening. He had heard that the Hereford and Gloucester canal was going to close to make way for the railway and so he embarked with a companion and his camera on a canoe expedition of the 34 miles of the canal waterway to capture pictures for posterity.

Alfred Watkins was born in Hereford and was an archaeologist and an inventor of photographic equipment. His fascination with photography began with a primitive pinhole camera which he made from a cigar box. He patented an 'exposure meter' which contributed greatly to photography's evolution as a mass-market art form. Some of his camera equipment and photographic archive are held by the Hereford Museum and Library Service.

The Hereford to Gloucester canal past, present and future.

The earliest plans for a canal linking Hereford through Ledbury with the River Severn to access the industrial Midlands, Bristol and the South-West were proposed in 1774. A much grander scheme connecting Stourport-on-Severn and Leominster were drawn up in 1777. In 1790 a revised plan provided a branch to the coal fields of Newent and was submitted to Parliament.

By 1795 a tunnel was under construction at Oxenhall to provide access to Newent. However, the tunnel proved difficult to construct and a considerable overspend was experienced. The grand opening of the canal was reported in the Hereford Journal of the 4th April 1798: 'the banks of the canal were lined with spectators who hailed the boats with reiterated acclamations'. Around 2000 people lined the banks and wharf in New Street. The celebrations continued with a dinner held at the George Inn. It was recorded that 'Coals of the finest quality are now delivered to the Wharf at 13s 6d – the former price was 24s per ton'. The wharf described here is at the southern end of New Street close to where the Full Pitcher pub is sited next to the A417 and A449 roundabout. Today there is no physical evidence of the wharf to be seen.

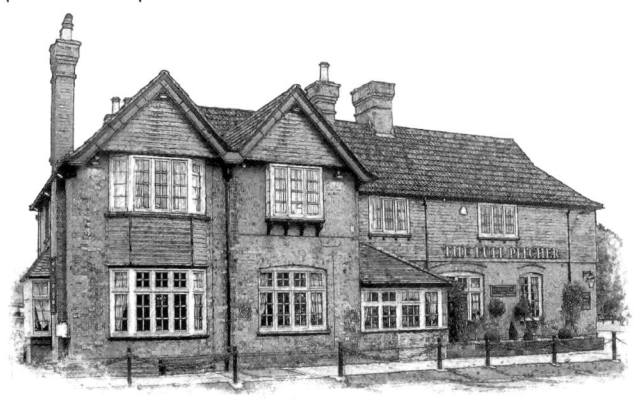

Ledbury was the only market town in the county to enjoy a canal link with the outside world. By 1812 the income for the canal had doubled since 1804 and the Canal Company had £1,200 in the bank. In 1827 local man, Stephen Ballard was appointed as Clerk to the Canal Company and after much deliberation a revised route to Hereford was planned. Work started in 1839 with the section to Bye Street completed in 1840. The final section to the Hereford basin was finished in 1845.

By 1858 the canal carried 47,560 tons of goods. However the steel rails of the developing railway network were fast approaching. The beginning of the end came in 1862 when the canal was leased to the Great Western and West Midland Railway. The railway company kept the canal going, but half the canal was closed in 1881 when the Ledbury to Gloucester railway was built by the Great Western and West Midland Railway Company. Subsequently the rest of the canal system went into disuse.

The present day Herefordshire and Gloucestershire Canal Trust has the aim of 'completing the full restoration of the canal from Gloucester to Hereford', a distance of 34 miles. Volunteers have reinstated the towpath at Dymock and stretches of the canal at Monkhide, Yarkhill, Aylestone and Oxenhall.

The stone chamber of House Lock at Oxenhall has also been completely restored.

The completion of the Ledbury section and further progress at Dymock, would allow Herefordshire and Gloucestershire to be joined by a stretch of navigable canal for the first time since the Victorian days.

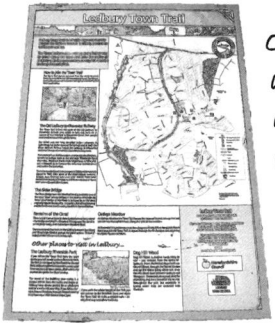

Our route takes us along the former canal and railway line. The embankment continues alongside the playing fields to the right. This is a very popular route with local dog walkers. The track now climbs slightly as the first road to be crossed is encountered. A very narrow single track footbridge spans the road below. The embankment following the footbridge is now much higher than the houses to the left and right. The trees either side of the embankment are mostly deciduous and therefore due to the leaf cover there is not much to see during the summer months.

If we were able to look up towards the town onto the main road named the Homend which runs from the Market House to Ledbury Station, there is a large Victorian house next to the more recent Tesco supermarket. This is where the budding Poet Laureate, John Masefield lived. It was named the Knapp and was built by his father Edward Masefield. With its extensive gardens and orchard it would have had in those days an unobstructed view of the canal and its redevelopment into a railway line.

A second Ledbury Town Trail information board comes into view. The path is easy

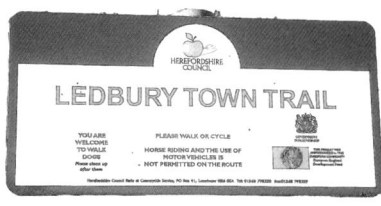

going and now curves towards the outskirts of the town. It then follows a brick built bridge over the Hereford Road which is known as the Skew Bridge at map reference SO 70626 38313. This is the most angled or skewed bridge across any road in the County. Shortly after the bridge, the current Birmingham to Hereford railway line comes into view, the path now drops down to the Hereford Road.

Ledbury Railway Station is just a short distance ahead. A sadly dilapidated information board is located alongside the footpath. Our route leads towards the railway station by crossing the Bromyard Road, the B214.

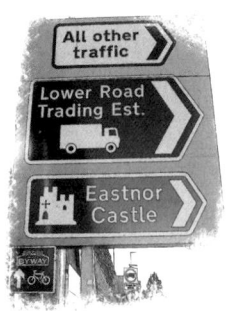

There is an opportunity to visit the station where the ticket office has been adorned with railway memorabilia, or alternatively head away from town towards the Bromyard Road Industrial Estate adjacent to and under the railway bridge.

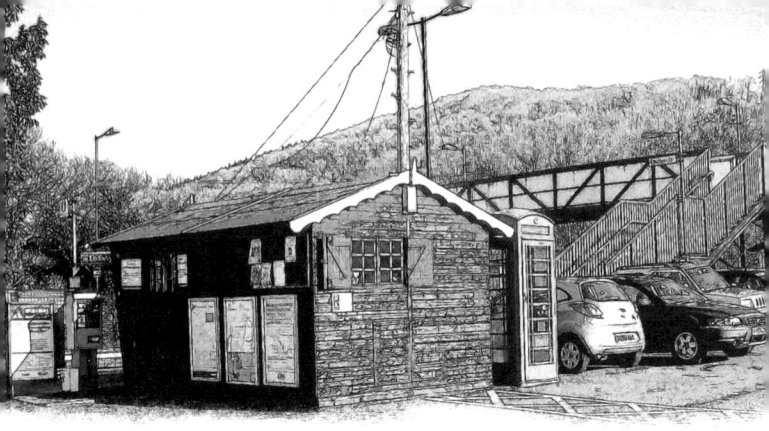

Very shortly on the right, tucked away in the hedgerow a footpath sign indicates the route at map reference SO 70703 38614.

After crossing over the only stile of the walk, the footpath heads uphill with a cider apple orchard to the left and the field boundary to the right and further over

the railway cutting.
The hedgerow supports a large
number of rabbits and other
wildlife.

The path continues uphill into
the next field, into view comes
the modern looking Frith Wood House which is
owned by the Forestry Commission. Looking
back down the route taken, the Bromyard Road

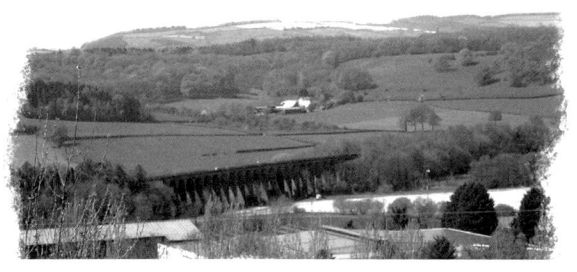

Industrial Estate is in the foreground but
further on is the impressive Ledbury railway
viaduct spanning 372 yards across the flood
plain of the Leadon Valley.
Carrying on, a short uphill stretch through a
small copse leads to
a swing gate with a
bent bar and then onto
a tarmac driveway
at map reference SO
71124 38668.

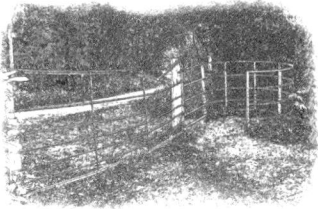

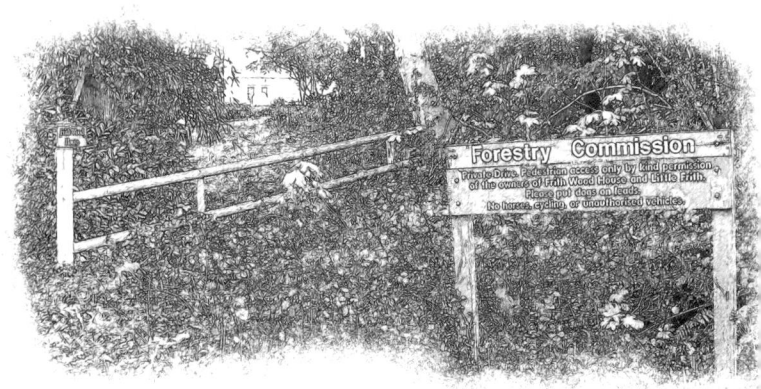

The route now heads downhill away from the Forestry Commission 'no entry sign'.

The panoramic landscape of the Herefordshire

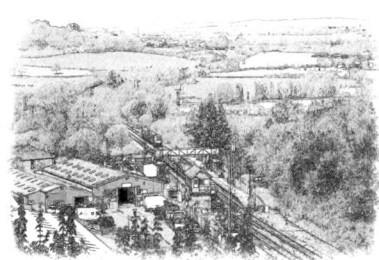

countryside and Ledbury Railway Station opens out above the entrance to the 1,323 yard long Ledbury railway tunnel.

Ledbury was finally connected to the railway network in 1861. Both the county towns of Hereford and Worcester were already linked to the fast developing railway network. Hereford was connected to the ports and industry of South Wales by the Newport, Abergavenny

& Hereford Railway Company. To the east Worcester was joined to the capital via Oxford and to the West Midlands, with the formation of the Oxford, Worcester & Wolverhampton Railway Company. These two companies looked to complete this east-west link through Malvern and Ledbury and formed the West Midlands Railway Company. Parliament granted them permission for the construction of the Worcester to Hereford line in 1853. A section of the line between Henwick (St John's in Worcester), Malvern and Colwall was constructed and in use by 1859. The Hereford section opened in 1861. The Ledbury to Gloucester railway line opened in 1885 and had stations and halts at Ledbury Halt (Bye Street), Dymock, Newent, Over Junction and Gloucester. In 1959 the line was closed to passenger traffic. Ledbury Station was called Ledbury Junction from 1885 to 1959. The 27 mile stretch of railway line between the two county towns spans the Leadon Valley with an impressive viaduct together with a long tunnel between Ledbury and Colwall and a further tunnel between

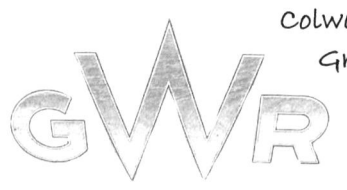

Colwall and Malvern. The Great Western Railway Company acquired the West Midlands Railway Company which to this day provides the service between Hereford and London.

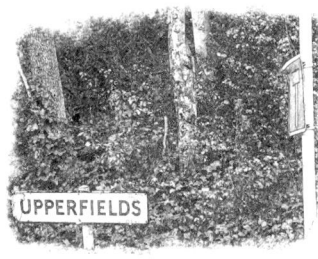

The road now joins the busy Knapp Lane. Opposite, there is a footpath leading into Dog Hill Wood. Our intention is to maintain the views across the Leadon valley and walk across the road. A little to the right is the single lane, no-through road called Upperfields (appropriate name).

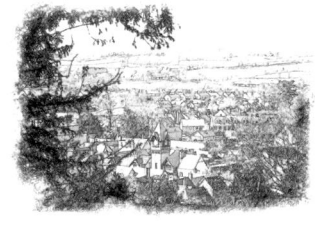

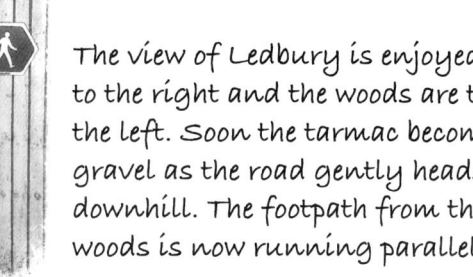

The view of Ledbury is enjoyed to the right and the woods are to the left. Soon the tarmac becomes gravel as the road gently heads downhill. The footpath from the woods is now running parallel to the track so deviate a little uphill and continue to follow the footpath, which is adorned with Bluebells in May.

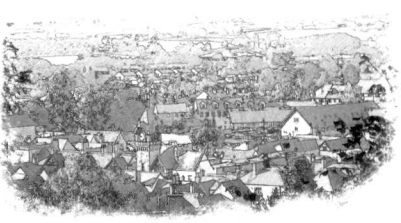

Upperfields comes to an abrupt end with a small track heading downhill which is ignored at map reference SO 71225 38637. Our footpath runs parallel with the hedge giving good views across Ledbury.

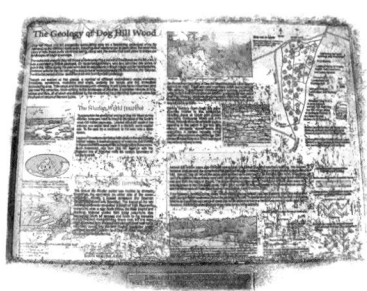

The large fermentation tanks of the Heineken brewery can be seen in the distance plus the rather more attractive facets of Ledbury town in the foreground. A rather scruffy signboard is soon encountered describing the 'Geology of Dog Hill Wood'.

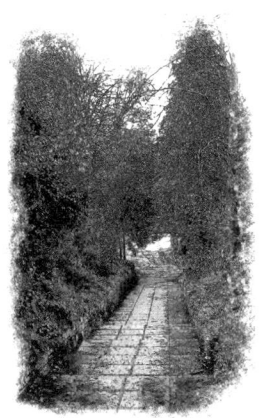

The path now descends quite steeply and is joined from the left by another from Dog Hill Wood.

At the time of the Domesday Survey this footpath was the original drovers route to Malvern. After a short steep decent, concrete steps lead onto the quiet Church Street. Just before the steps end, on the wall to the left is a small plaque indicating that this was once called 'Green Lane. The old packhorse route to Worcester'.

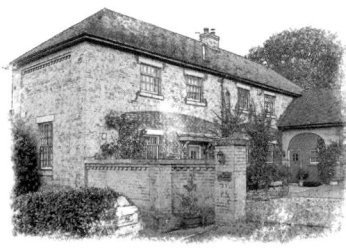

Continue a little way downhill and on the left is the Georgian styled Coach House which is part of the Upperhall Estate.

To the left is the small gateway leading into the Walled Garden and the churchyard of Ledbury Parish Church of St Michael and All Angels at map reference SO 71201 38154.

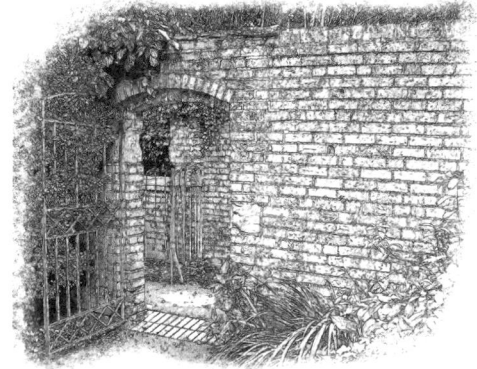

However, if you enjoy reading the local history plaques for which there are many in Ledbury, fifty or so metres further down on the right, following the line of an old stone wall is a row of modern houses. On the first house there is the interesting round plaque 'Ants' Nest Demolished 1973'. The history behind such an unusual name appears to have been recorded in the book 'Old Ledbury By An Octogenarian' written by George Wargent in 1889.

A carpenter was working on the construction of the original properties and said to the owner of the building company "this will be a regular ants nist gaffer". From that remark the name has remained ever since. The keen eyed will also notice the original grammatical error with the word Ant's. The original apostrophe is now overpainted.

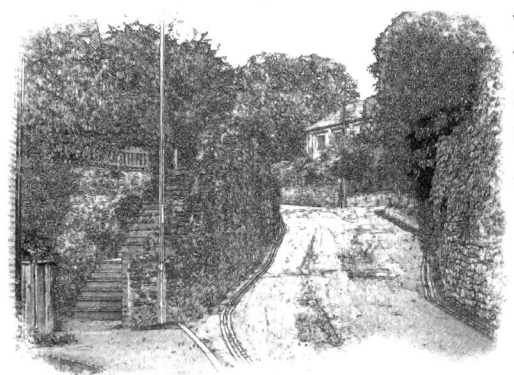

Walk back up the road and into the gateway where once there was a swing gate.

Take the immediate right archway into the delightful Walled Garden and downhill

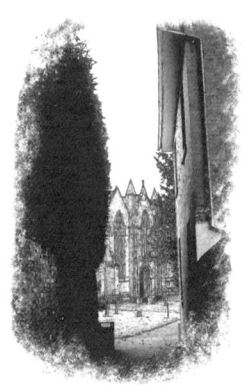

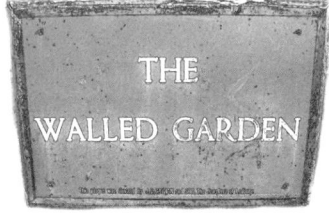

towards the gate and the remarkable 16th century black and white timbered Church House and the Abbots Lodge dating back to 1480 which was once the vicarage and is next to the walled churchyard in Church Lane.

The church is covered in more detail in the Ledbury Town Centre Heritage walk.

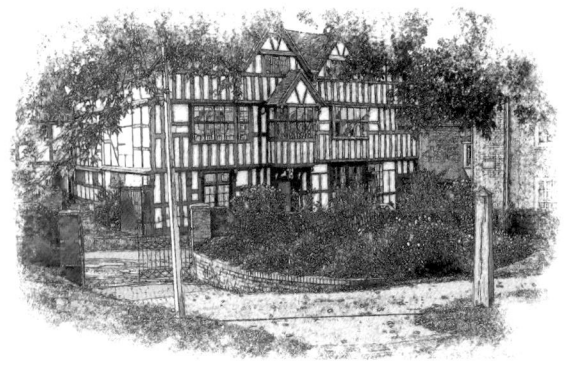

On leaving the secluded Walled Garden the impressive 18th century Georgian style 'Old Magistrates House' is slightly off to the right.

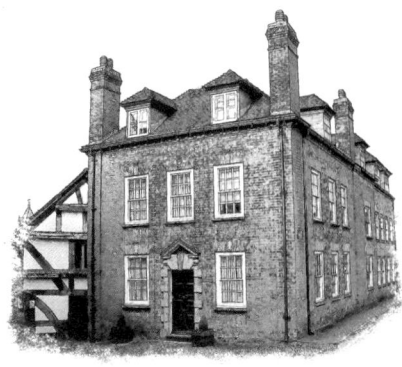

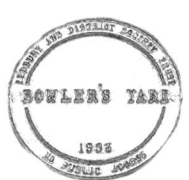

Look up to see the plaque describing that these buildings were restored in 1987-88.

We continue our walk along the original Ledbury to Malvern route down Church Street. Whilst Church Street does not appear on many picture

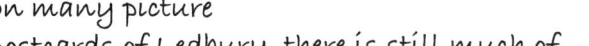

postcards of Ledbury, there is still much of interest to be seen. On the right are the former White Hart public house and the Bowler's Yard 1933 plaque.

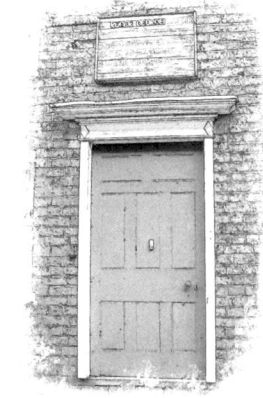

Just a little further on is an interesting feature with the 'Ledbury Station brickworks' brick set at chest height.

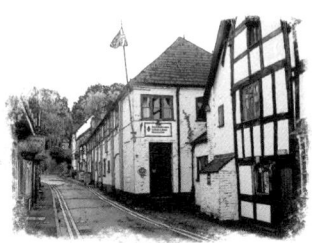

On the opposite side is the rear of the Prince of Wales public house. The British Legion Club and its Union Jack fluttering in the wind is next and on the corner is the information board for the 16th century Painted Room on the early Tudor structure of the Town Council Offices.

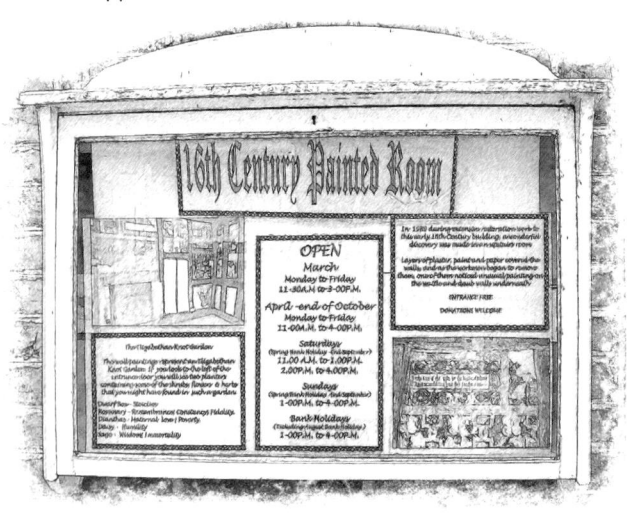

During restoration in 1989 a number of fascinating 16th century wall paintings were discovered. Just a few steps further on brings us to the original crossroads known as Lower Cross next to the Market House.

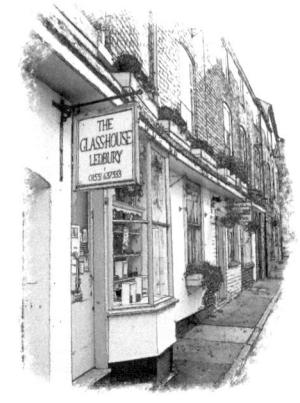

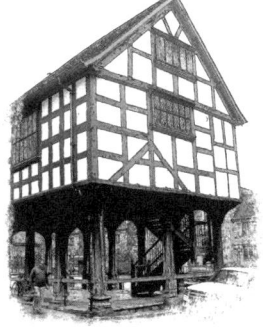

The Upper Cross is now the one-way junction of New Street, the A449 Worcester-Malvern Road next to the imposing Ledbury Park House.

The tall Elizabeth Barrett Browning Institute building built in 1892 is on the opposite side of the road on the corner of Bye Street, which brings us to within shouting distance of our starting point. Thus concluding this short history of public transport inspired excursion around the delightful market town of Ledbury.

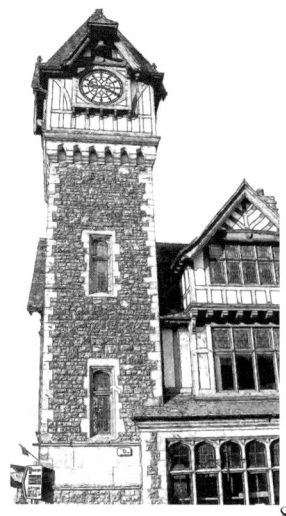

Notes and observations from the walk

Chapter 4

Walk 3

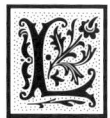edbury town centre to Eastnor Castle circular walk

Summary

This delightful circular walk from Ledbury town centre to Eastnor Castle experiences the rich historical legacy of the Herefordshire countryside. The walk will take three hours without refreshment stops or time spent visiting the 19th century mock castle and grounds. To enter the castle grounds, the opening times are from Easter until the last Sunday in September. Opening times are extended from Sunday to Thursdays in late July through to August. Opening times to the castle are not so extensive and so it is best to check in advance of your visit. There are plenty of events taking place at the castle which are worth looking out for. For further information see the website www.eastnorcastle.com

It is best to wear walking boots for this excursion. The footpaths through the woodlands and fields will make it very difficult to use buggies. There are four kissing gates, one stile and one five-barred gate to navigate. The wildlife likely to be encountered is in the form of pheasants a plenty.

Refreshments
Other than the hostelries and tea shops in abundance in Ledbury town centre the only other opportunity, just for a few months in the year is the small ice cream stall located in Eastnor Castle's car park. Once in the grounds of the castle there is an excellent tea room and cafe.

Wells, springs and spouts
A small spout close to the entrance of the footpath leading into Coneygree Woods from the Worcester Road.

Eastnor village green well but alas no water.

Places and points of interest
The Market House, Ledbury Park, Eastnor Church, Eastnor Castle and grounds.

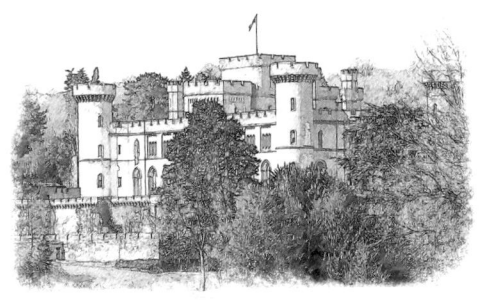

Height map

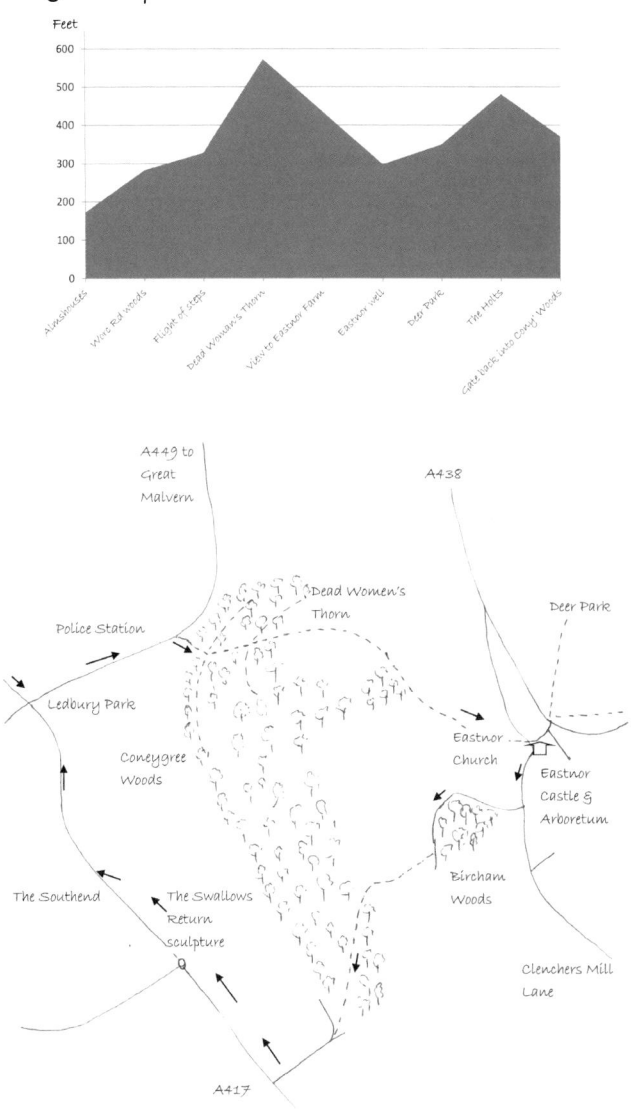

Connections to other walks.
Walk 11 Hollybush to Eastnor Castle returning by the Ridgeway Path. From 'A Pictorial Guide to the Malvern Hills', Book 3.

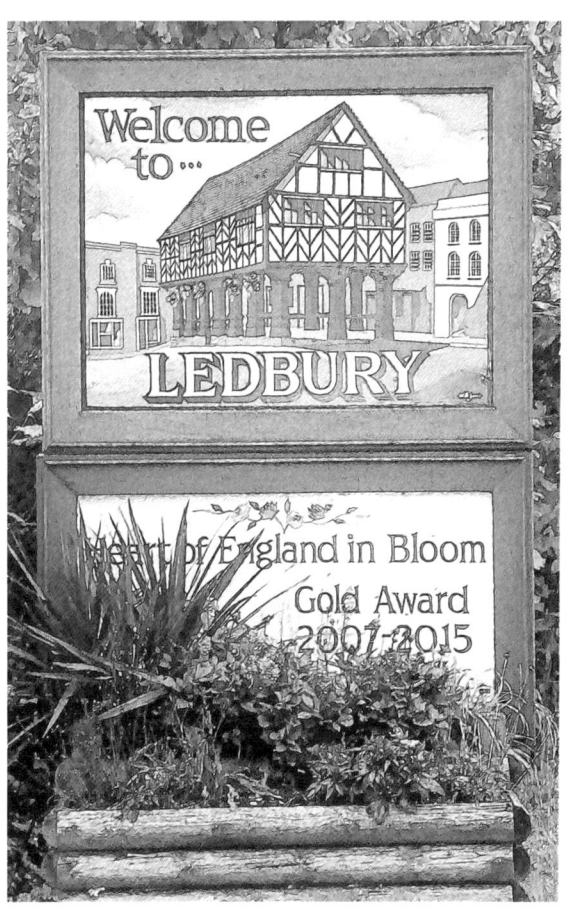

The Walk

A central location in Ledbury to start this walk is the attractive Market House which was built in the 1640's. This Ledbury icon stands on sixteen oak pillars cut from the Malvern Forest and is located at map reference SO 71091 37687.

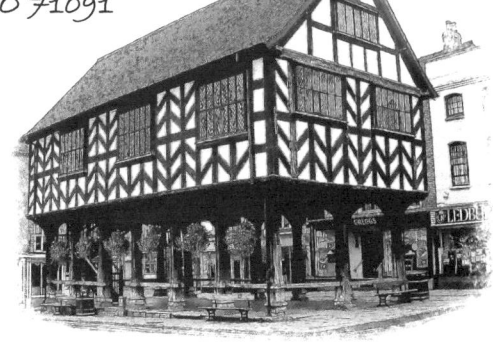

Now venture towards the crossroads near the 16th century Feathers Hotel, on the way spend some time window shopping from the range of interesting local retailers, including the two bookshops which stock copies of my books!

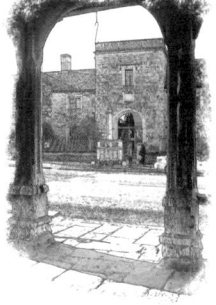

On reaching the crossroads take the turning signposted A449 Malvern. This was until the 19th century known as Horse Lane and is now

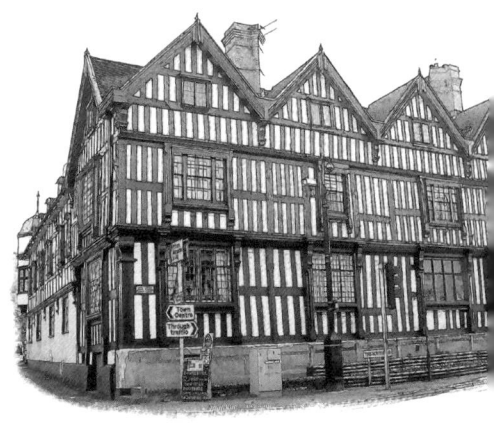

designated the Worcester Road. On the opposite side of the road, is the impressive black and white Ledbury Park House which was built by Edward Skinner, circa 1595. Originally it was named New House. Pevsner in 1963 described it as 'the grandest black and white house in the county'. The archives tell us that it was Prince Rupert's headquarters during the battle of Ledbury in 1645. Later on it became the home of the Biddulph family from 1688-1941. Their family tree included the Deputy Lieutenant of Herefordshire, Members of Parliament and marriage into the Prime Minister, Robert Peel's family.

Walking away from the cross-roads take extra care as the footpath is quite narrow. Continue past the impressive looking Priory Lodge and Priory Gatehouse which is set back from the road.

The Ledbury Guide of 1824 describes this as 'Mr Dunn's Academy'. Young gentleman were boarded and carefully instructed in every branch of commercial, nautical, mathematical and classical education. Continue past the 1950's Police Station on the left. Just a short distance along the footpath on the opposite side of the road a footpath sign can be seen. Three small steps down the bank provide access to the road, near a row of parked cars (unless you are enjoying this walk early in the morning). Cross the busy Worcester Road to the footpath sign and the private entrance to Coneygree.

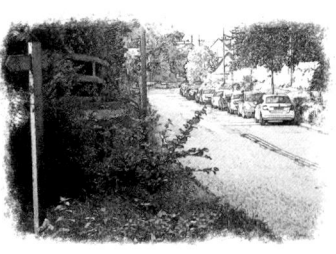

Note the tiny sign indicating the route to Eastnor. This is the start of the off-road section. As can be observed the footpath begins its uphill climb into Coneygree Woods next to the house called 'Eastwood' at map reference SO 71235 37818. The name Conegree has its origins in the term 'coney' which is a rabbit warren. During the 13th century the rabbit was much valued for its fur and meat.

The footpath lies in a deep gully and climbs quite steeply through the woods and can be quite muddy if the weather has been inclement. Rather strangely, I have also been faced with a torrent of water cascading towards the road when it has not been particularly wet, so be warned! During the summer the tree canopy makes the ascent rather gloomy. On reaching the first fork in the path, continue to the left where there is a modern clay spout which is responsible for the deluge of water. Walk towards the long flight of steps which ascend to a broad woodland track. The flight of steep steps is at map reference SO 71702 37701. Continue uphill over the track.

From the shape and general feel of the path which is more noticeable at the higher end of the woods it becomes obvious that this is the ancient track described in various maps between Ledbury and Eastnor. The route then crosses another wider track with a smaller flight of steps. Continue a short distance uphill through the woods and a new shiny galvanised swing gate provides entry into the open fields beyond.

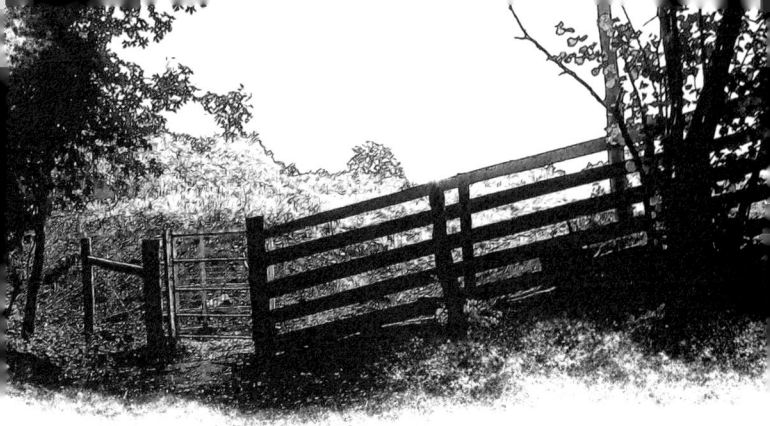

The path is clearly marked by the footpath sign. The woods are to the left as our route heads towards 'Dead Womans Thorn' as indicated on the OS Explorer Map 190 Malvern Hills & Bredon Hill. In Victorian times this was called 'Deddymans Thorn'. So any reference to a woman hanging herself on a Thorn tree, as I noticed on one particular website is pure nonsense. However, who or what Deddyman was and whether or not he died is still unclear! If you have any knowledge on this subject then please email me at info@malvernwalks.co.uk

The path exits the field where another new gate this time of the five barred variety at map reference SO 72068 37707 can be found. The route

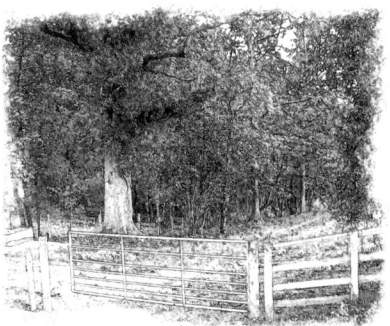

is straight on and crosses a track, which as can be seen on the map eventually leads to Hill Farm. At various times of the year there are substantial numbers of pheasants wandering about as only pheasants do. The large pheasant population in this corner of Herefordshire is due to breeding for the 'driven pheasant shooting' which is held in the Eastnor estate for around 25 days each year. According to 'The Field' website there are 30 drives to shoot and for each pheasant shot a payment of £36 plus VAT is required!

Continue along the edge of the next field and on the left tucked away amongst the trees is a ramshackle building. A little further on the view opens out with British Camp prominent in the distance.

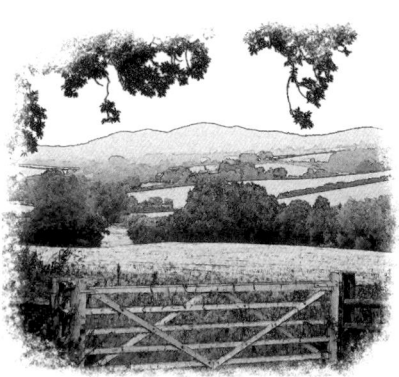

The path heads down to the left (north) corner. The footpath sign indicates the route through another new galvanised swing gate.

The path now follows the route of a designated vehicle track. Every few moments the silence is shattered by a daft pheasant making a bid for freedom out of the undergrowth. The contours of the hillside are downhill from left to right. Following, there is a very short downhill stretch through the corner of the woods which is indicated on the map as Eastnor Hill. On exiting the wood the view ahead is quite panoramic with a glimpse of Eastnor Castle tucked away in the trees behind the farm buildings, alas with their not so attractive stainless steel silos. To the left is the church of St John the Baptist Eastnor and in the distance British Camp, this is at map reference SO 72701 37214.

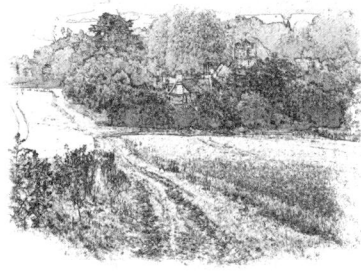

Heading downhill the ground levels out when reaching the hedgerow separating the churchyard from the footpath. This first section of the walk will have taken around 45 minutes at a gentle pace. The pheasants are now more abundant than seagulls on a school playground following break time.

The footpath continues to the left of the churchyard. The golden cockerel weathervane on the church spire will be glinting if sunny and to the left is a football pitch with a heavily biased gradient.

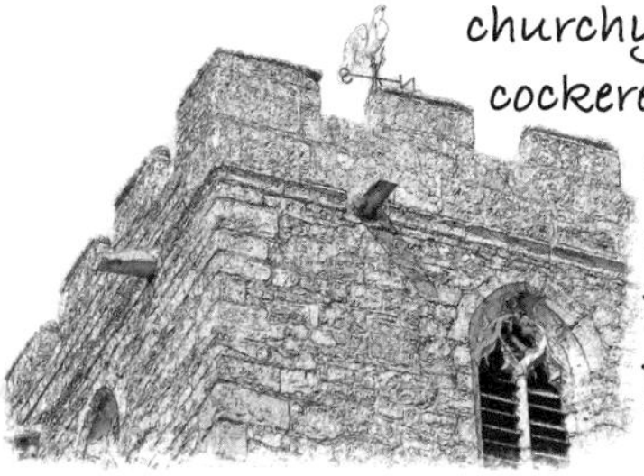

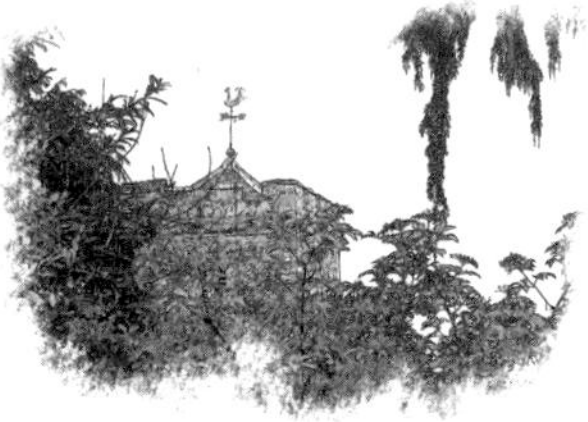

A couple of steps lead down to Upper Road, the minor road connecting the A438 Eastnor village, castle and onto Bromsberrow and Clenchers Mill.

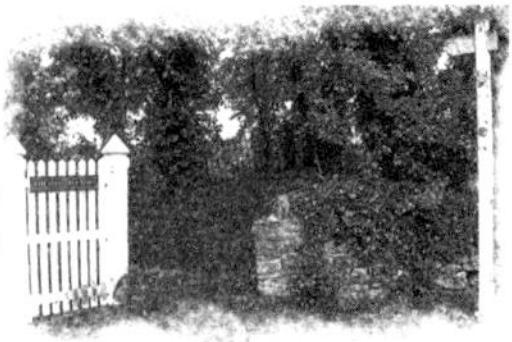

Turning to the right, the attractive Lychgate, churchyard and scenic backdrop provides the archetypal setting of an English country church.

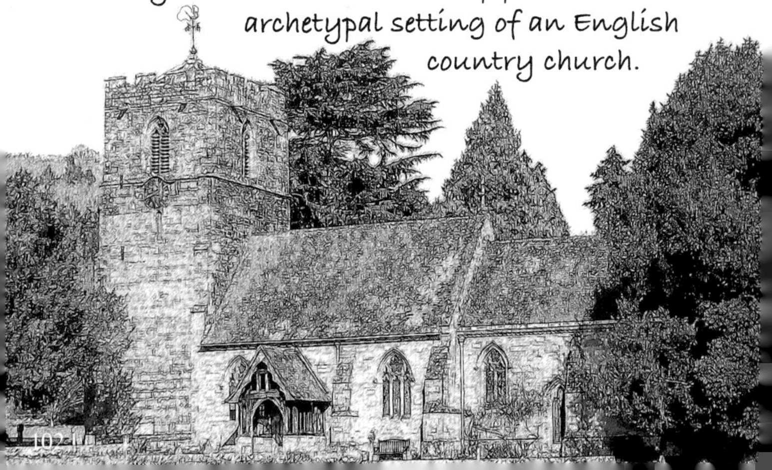

The tower is thought to date back to the fourteenth century. The rest of the church was redesigned by Sir George Gilbert Scott and was taken down in 1851, and rebuilt the following year. As can be seen, the stonework is clearly different between the tower and the main body of the church. It is well worth a visit inside to look at the ornate Somers Cox Mortuary Chapel in the North East corner of the Nave.

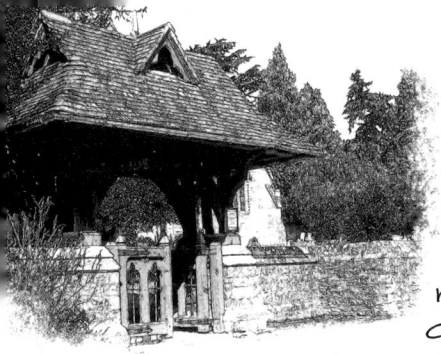

On leaving the churchyard to the right there is a delightful village green. Eastnor Primary school is to the left. Ahead on the well tended grass there is an attractively constructed early twentieth century brick built grade II listed well housing constructed for Lady Somers of Eastnor.

The Italian Renaissance styled terracotta reliefs provide a misleading inscription above the well basin as there is no opportunity for anyone to quench their thirst!

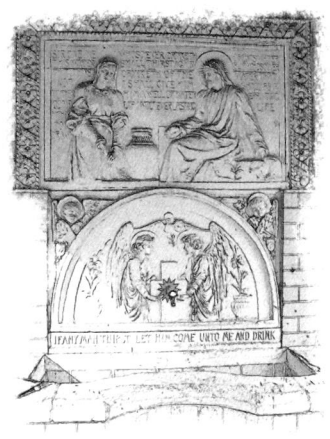

The inscription reads:-
'So give me this water
that I thirst not neither come hither to draw
drink Drinkith who so ever drinketh of the water
Water springing up into everlasting life
Let him thirst let him come unto me and drink
Water spring up into everlasting life'.
The well housing is at map reference SO 73203

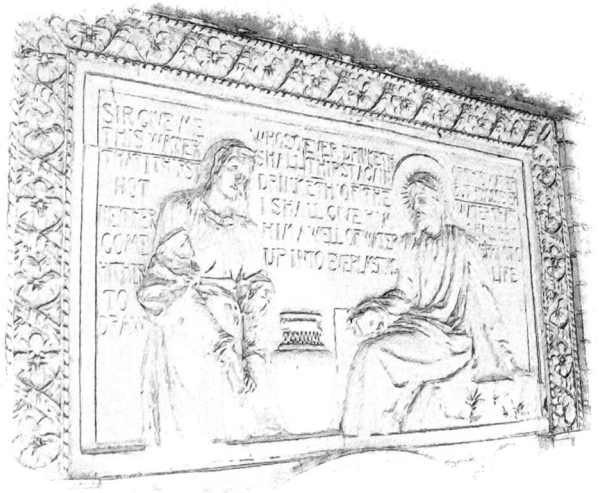

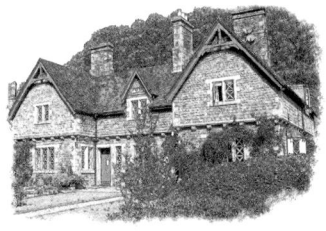
To the right of the school is a brick Georgian styled semi-detached house and a little further down is the picturesque black and white thatched cottage which was once the Eastnor Post Office which has since been converted to a family home.

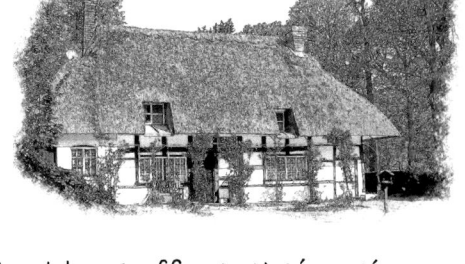
If the castle grounds are closed, a great view of the castle can be achieved by walking past the old post office to the junction of the A438 and crossing over the road into the Deer Park. For a quick view, head to the right parallel with the road (the picture shown here), or if more time is available then walk up the single track lane which climbs up the side of the valley for a more elevated view at map reference SO 7378 3719.

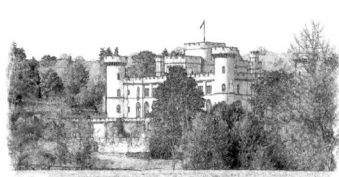
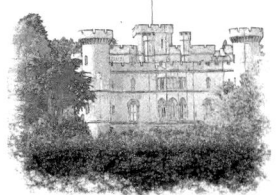

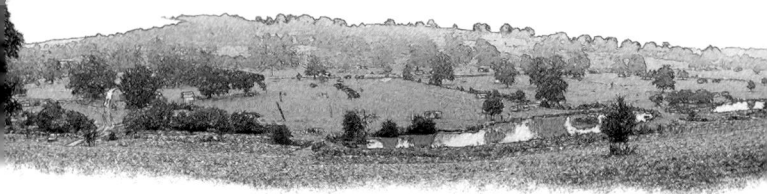

The Deer Park opens up as a caravan, camper van and tent site during the summer months. It is also used for large outdoor concerts such as Lakefest.

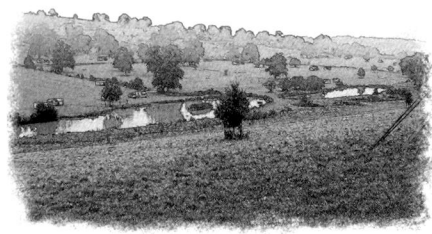

On the return journey do note the impressive wrought iron gates to the Eastnor Castle lodge.

From the green, turn to the right and head towards the castle along Clenchers Mill Lane.

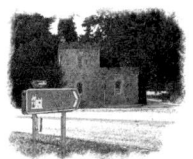

The lane originally formed part of the boundary between the Bishop of Hereford's estate and Gilbert de Claire's chase. The Eastnor Estate office and Eastnor Pottery are to the right. The Land Rover Experience and castle entrance and car park is a little further on to the left.

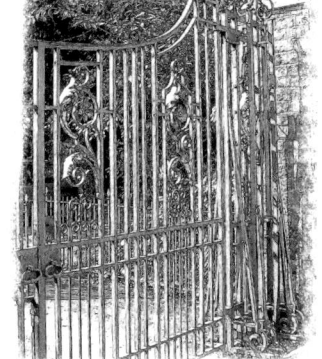

If it is open, there is an opportunity to visit this 19th century mock castle and grounds. The Arboretum and landscaped grounds with the Lakeland walk provide much to see for the keen horticulturist. For the younger age group there is an excellent play area complete with obstacle course, tree top walk and maze. For refreshments there is an excellent café, 'The Old Kitchen Tea Room' serves a wide range of foods and beverages and there is also an ice cream parlour.

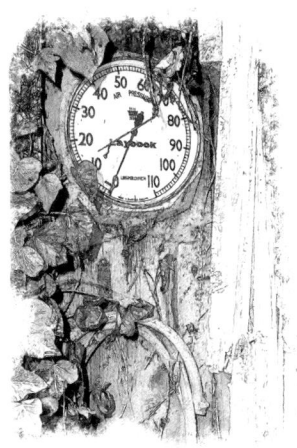

The Eastnor cricket ground is opposite the castle entrance. Our return journey leads back down the lane, take the single track road leading to the entrance of the Eastnor Pottery centre and Eastnor Estate Farm. Do look out for the antique air hose made by Laycock, which

was probably used for vehicle tyres many years ago. It is located on the corner amongst the ivy as the road turns to the left.

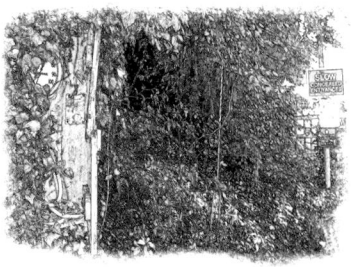

Eastnor Estate Farm is to the right opposite the pottery centre.

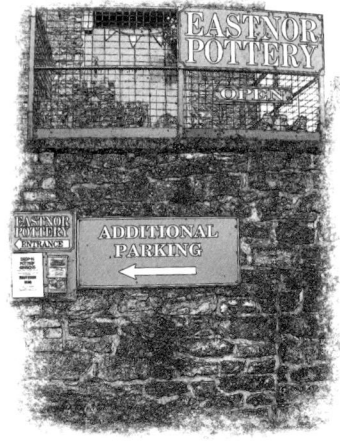

The track is also a bridleway and appears to be well used. Continue uphill skirting the edge of Bircham's Wood. Over to the right is a view of the hillside which was traversed earlier. Several tracks lead deeper into the woods, our route follows the single vehicle width track. A little further on to the right the footpath sign indicates a diagonal route across the field with 'The Holts' buildings on the skyline.

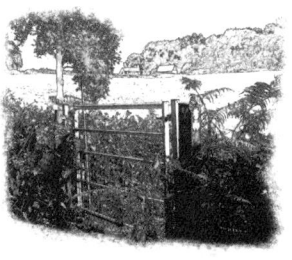

The path does in fact cut through the grounds of the Holts at map reference SO 72546 36692. The footpath now joins a single track which leads downhill towards a five barred gate, shortly before the gate, the footpath turns off to the right with a view across a large field. The path crosses diagonally across the field leading back to Coneygree Woods.

Another new galvanised gate at map reference
SO 72248 36722 has been erected and after

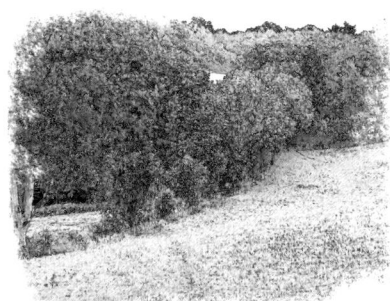

passing through it, the old wooden gate comes into view.

The footpath here amongst the trees can be quite muddy as it climbs up through the woods. The footpath then levels off making a right hand turn, which is clearly signposted. Ignore the footpath to the right which heads up to the centre of the woods. A few metres further on heading downhill, a right hand

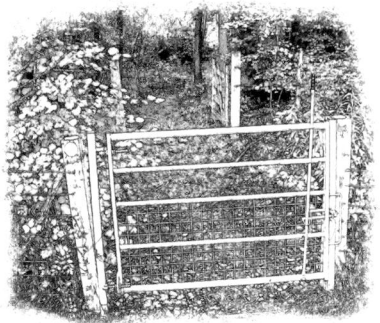

turn heads off to Bullens House. Our route is to head down the track towards the fairly busy A417. Fear not as not one step has to be taken on the main road as there are the remains of the old road which is now a rather suitable footpath running parallel to the A417 on a slightly elevated footing. An attractive recent addition to the roundabout is the metal sculpture named The Swallows Return. This was donated by Herefordshire sculpture Walenty Pytel. One of his commissions is the Silver Jubilee Fountain outside the Houses of Parliament and locally The Buzzards in Rose Bank Gardens in Great Malvern.

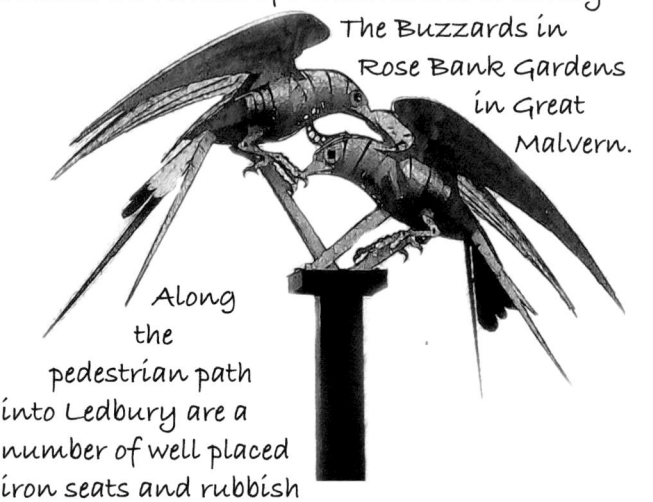

Along the pedestrian path into Ledbury are a number of well placed iron seats and rubbish bins. Reaching the roundabout, signposted Hereford A438 head back into Ledbury. The road is named Southend. On the right is the impressive house, Underdown, next door is the Ledbury tennis club and then Ledbury Park. The 'Underdown' name was recorded in the Ledbury Borough in 1288. On the opposite side of the road are the stylish Georgian three-storey town houses, the leisure centre and the John Masefield High School. The impressive Gloucester House nestles between quite an interesting mix of Edwardian, Victorian and older black and white cottages.

After passing the 16th century Royal Oak, moments later you are back in the centre of this delightful market town where a variety of refreshments or retail therapy can be enjoyed.

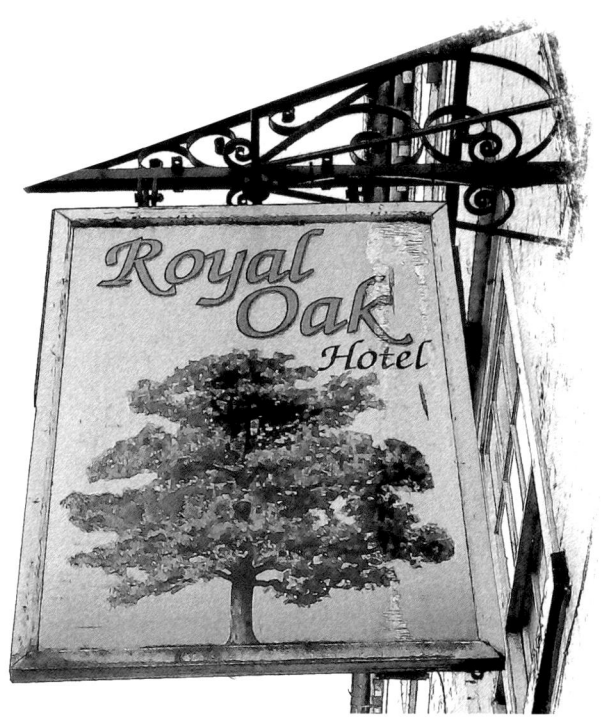

Notes and observations from the walk

Waypoints listing for each walk

Walk 1
An assumption has been made that since walk 1 is around the town centre no waypoints would be necessary!

Walk 2
Around Ledbury Town: a brief history of transport in Ledbury

SO 70828 37690
SO 70626 38313
SO 70703 38614
SO 70845 38678
SO 71124 38668
SO 71225 38637
SO 71201 38154

Walk 3
Ledbury town centre to Eastnor Castle circular walk

SO 71091 37687
SO 71702 37701
SO 72068 37707
SO 72701 37214
SO 73199 37182
SO 73785 37195
SO 72546 36692
SO 72248 36722

Health and Safety Information
Whilst the walks in the Pictorial Guide series have been checked, routes identified on public highways, bridleways and footpaths, no responsibility is accepted for any accidents however caused. No responsibility is given for any goods and property left at any location identified within these books.

Hostelries
Ledbury has many fine hostelries, the listing here does not signify any bias to a particular pub, equally if a hostelry has been missed out then that is purely an error on my part. The description in the main body of the book will have indicated where I have waxed lyrical over a particular establishment.

The Brewery Inn
Marstons
A traditional pub popular with the locals.
Bye Street, HR8 2AG.
Telephone 01531 634272

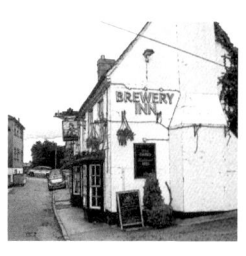

The Feathers
Independent
Ledbury's premier hotel
25 High Street, HR8 1DS.
Telephone 01531 635266
Outside to the rear there is a large walled garden and patio leading to the car park.

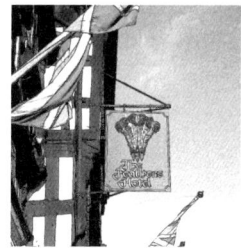

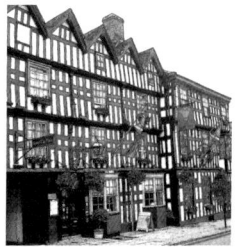

Horseshoe Inn
Enterprise Inns
The Homend, HR8 1BN.
Telephone 01531 632770
It has a delightful tiny beer garden to the rear. There are discounts for card carrying CAMRA members and it serves authentic home-made Hungarian food.

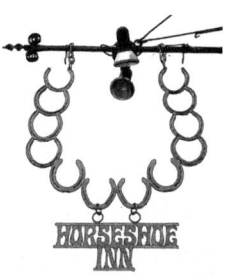

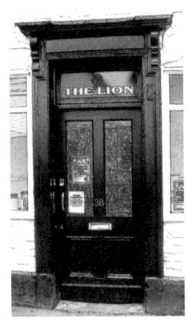

The Lion
Independent
38 Bye Street, HR8 2AA
A two-room microbrewery.

Prince of Wales
Independent
Church Lane, HR8 1DL. Telephone 01531 577001 Website www.powledbury.co.uk

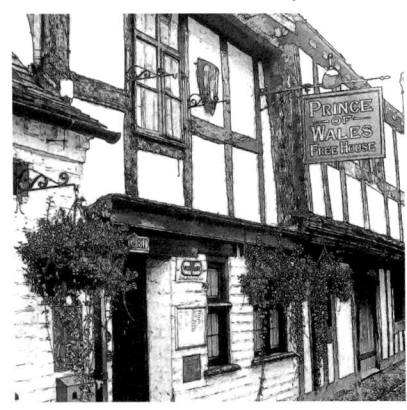

The Prince of Wales public house dates from the fifteenth or sixteenth century. It was Herefordshire CAMRA Pub of the Year 2013. The lunch menu supports the local butcher DT Waller & Sons . A great range of real ales with Hobson's and other classic local ales and ciders are available.

The Retreat Enterprise Inns
7 High Street, HR8 1DS.
Telephone 01531 635142

Beer garden to the rear of the pub and serves a wide range of food.

The Royal Oak
Richmondhill Breweries Ltd
The Southend,
HR8 2EY.
Telephone 01531 248330
An old coaching inn, built in 1643 and renovated in 1890.

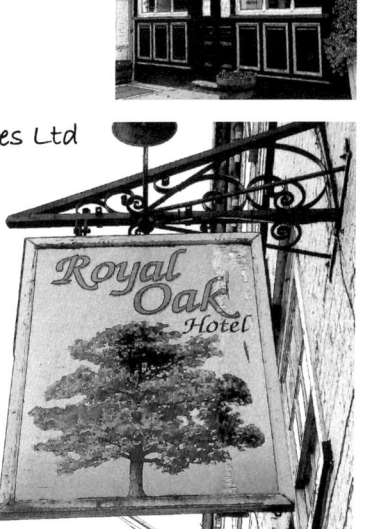

THE ROYAL OAK
1420 - REAR PART OF BUILDING CONSTRUCTED, USED AS A CIDER HOUSE.
1520 - FRONT PART BUILT AS SEPARATE HOUSE, USED AS ACCOMMODATION.
1645 - THE BUILDINGS JOINED TOGETHER AND USED AS A COACHING INN.
1856 - BRICK FACADE ADDED TO THE FRONT AND ALL EXPOSED INTERIOR BEAMS COVERED UP.
1998 - RESTORED AS NEAR AS POSSIBLE TO ITS ORIGINAL STATE.

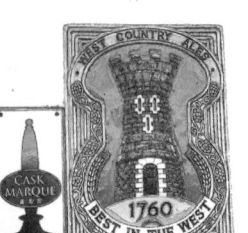

Seven Stars
Independent
11 The Homend. HR8 1BN.
Telephone 01531 635800
Website www.sevenstarsledbury.co.uk
The pub underwent a full renovation shortly before this book was printed. The pub food is supported by its own farm no less!

The Full Pitcher
Independent
New Street (far end near the ring road). HR8 2EN.
Telephone 01531 632352
A large family friendly pub recently refurbished.

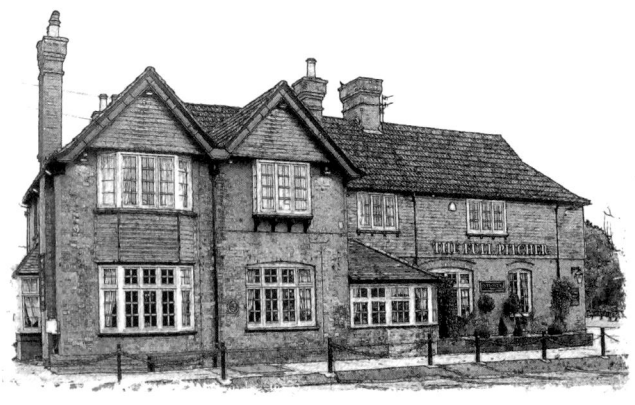

The Talbot Hotel
Wadworths
14 New Street,
HR8 2DX.
Telephone 01531 632963.
Website www.talbotledbury.co.uk

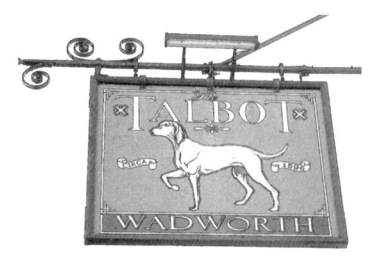

This is a former coaching inn with some ghostly history connected to the English Civil War. It has the original oak panelled dining room with its fine carved over-mantle.

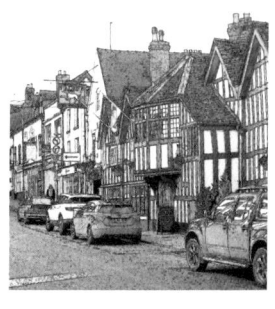

Further afield
The Wellington Inn
Independent
Chances Pitch (located on the main road between British Camp and Ledbury) Colwall. WR13 6HW
Telephone 01684 540269.
The pub was busy on a Monday lunchtime, I think that says a lot!

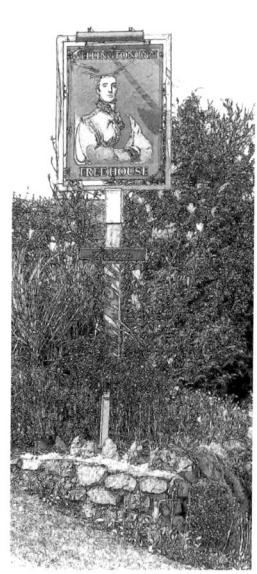

Westons Cider
The Bounds, Much Marcle, Ledbury, HR8
2NQ. Telephone 01531 660233.
Website www.westons-cider.co.uk

The Westons Cider Mill Tours take place at
11.00am, 12.30pm, 2.00pm and 3.30pm.

The Visitor Centre, Cider Shop, Restaurant and
Tea Room are open daily.

Bibliography
Books, magazines, leaflets and maps

Gavin Robinson S.F. A History and Description of Ledbury Parish Church. 1990.

Gavin Robinson S.F. The History of Butcher Row, Ledbury. 1981.

Gavin Robinson S.F. A Short History of the Parish of Ledbury, Herefordshire. 1980.

Hereford & Ross-On-Wye 189 Ordnance Survey Explorer Map. 2015.

Hillaby, Joe. Ledbury A Medieval Borough. Ledbury and District Trust Ltd in collaboaration with Logaston Press. 2005.

Ledbury Heritage Trail. Ledbury & District Civic Society leaflet.

Malvern Hills & Bredon Hill 190 Ordnance Survey Explorer Map 2007.

Malvern Gazette and Ledbury Reporter, October 11, 2013.

Masefield, John. The Ledbury Scene. Reprodux Printers, Hereford. Reprinted from the Original Edition of 1951.

St Katherine's Hospital and the Master's House leaflet.

The Heritage Centre (Old Grammar School) Church Lane, Ledbury leaflet 2015.

Watkins, Alfred. The Old Straight Track. Abacus 1974.
Woodcock, Roy. Walks Around The Malverns. Meridian 2005.

Websites
Eastnor Castle www.eastnorcastle.com

Herefordshire Council   www.herefordshire.gov.uk

Ledbury Civic Society   www.ledburycivicsociety.org

Ledbury History Society   www.ledburyhistorysociety.co.uk

Ledbury Library. Telephone 01432 383499.   www.herefordshire.gov.uk/libraries

Ledbury Parish Church www.ledburyparishchurch.org.uk

Ledbury Reporter www.ledburyreporter.co.uk/news

Ledbury Tourist Information www.visitorlinks.com

The Old-Ledbury Website is a fascinating collection of photographs and archives. It describes itself as a 'trip down memory lane between 1900's and the 1970's'. www.old-ledbury.co.uk

Equipment used to create this Guide
Garmin Etex hand held GPS
Olympus WS-300M voice recorder
Olympus C-310 digital camera
Asus Eee PC 900
Samsung R530 laptop
Akvis software

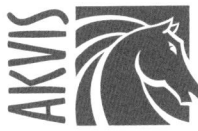

Contributors and acknowledgements
Colin Soley
Justine Sissons
Joshua Flint
Su Savage
Stuart Diplock

The Pictorial Guide series

Carl Flint's passion for writing about the world he travelled began with updates in the 'Lonely Planet' guides whilst trekking in India, Nepal and Bhutan. More recently 'Worcestershire Life' and 'All About Malvern' have published his work. Besides jogging and walking he also likes to cook and has contributed to 'The Little Book of Soups and Stews', compiled and edited by Dr Cyril Edwards. ISBN 9780956349101.

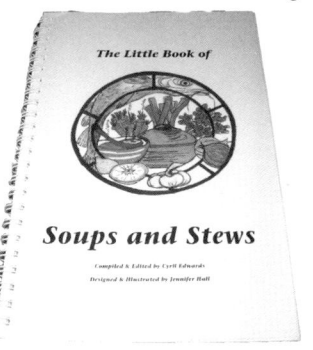

Titles available in the 'Pictorial Guides'
A Pictorial Guide to the Malvern Hills. Book 1: North Malvern, West Malvern and Malvern Link. Published July 2010.

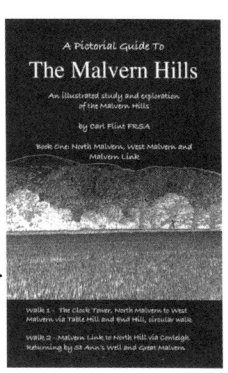

A Pictorial Guide to the Malvern Hills. Book 2: Great Malvern. Published December 2010.

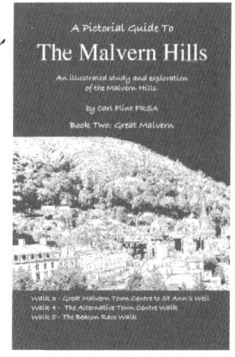

A Pictorial Guide to the Malvern Hills. Book 3: Malvern Wells, Welland, Little Malvern, British Camp, Castlemorton Common, Hollybed Common and Whiteleaved Oak. Published July 2012.

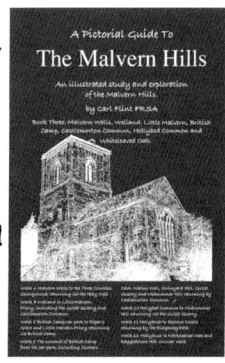

A Pictorial Guide to the Malvern Hills. Book 4: The Royal Well, Colwall and Alfrick Pound returning to the Dingle in West Malvern. Published July 2014.

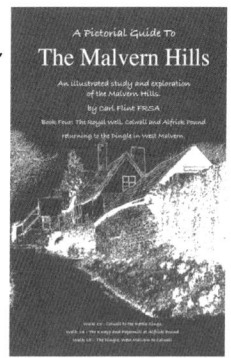

Index

A

Abbot's Lodge	47, 86
Abbot of Wigmore	24
Akvis	17
Almshouses	23, 26, 27, 28, 29, 70
Ansell, Harry	33
Ants' Nest	85
Aylestone	75

B

Badsey, Thomas	58
Bakers Dozen Cake Shop	71
Ballard, Stephen	75
Ballard, Thomas	50
Baylis, Thomas	28
Barrett Browning, Elizabeth	9
Barrett Browning Memorial Institute	29, 37, 89
Battle of Ledbury	65, 96
Belle Orchard	34
Biddulph, John	28, 51, 96
Bills Yard	37
Birmingham	13
Bircham's Wood	108
Bishop Hugo Foliot	23
Bishop of Hereford	10, 33, 43, 106
Bishop Robert de Bethune	18
Black Death	18
Blacksmith's Tomb	3, 57
Boat, The	72
Bosbury	32
Botticelli	55
Bowlers Yard	87
Brewery Inn	72, 115
Bristol	73
British Camp	11
British Legion club	88
Bromsberrow	102
Bromyard Road	77
Bromyard Road Industrial Estate	78, 79
Bullens House	109
Burgage Hall	45
Burgage plot	33, 34, 64
Butchers Row	28, 44
Butchers Row House Museum	29
Bye Street	18, 19, 29, 56, 70, 75, 89

C

Cabbage Lane	58

Captain Skinner see Skinner		E	
Carillon	49	Eastnor Castle & Deer Park	91, 101, 104, 107 103
Cathol	29		
Chapel Alley	63	Eastnor Church	102, 103
Chapter House	55	Eastnor Cricket Ground	107
Chez Pascal	44		
Church House		Eastnor Estate Farm	107
Church Lane	10, 29, 56	Eastnor Hill	101
Church Street	87	Eastnor Pottery	106
Codfather Part II	31	Edward III	18
Clenchers Mill Lane	102, 106	English Civil War	17, 50
Colwall	13, 81	Esso Garage	36
Common Garden Alley	37	Eastnor Post Office	105
		Eastnor Primary School	103
Coneygree Woods	92, 97, 108		
Cowper, Edward	24	Eastwood	98
Cupper, Theo	54		
		F	
D		Facebook	6
Dead Womans Thorn also known as Deddymans Thorn	99	Farmers Market	18
		Feathers Hotel	33, 64, 66, 95, 115
Design Quarter	61		
Dews Yard	36	Fire Brigade	71
Dog Hill Wood	82, 83	Forestry Commission	79, 80
Domesday Book	48, 84	Fox Lane	32
Dunn's Academy	59, 97	Frith Wood House	79
Dymock	75, 76	Full Pitcher Public House	74, 118

G

George Inn	74
Gilbert de Claire	106
Gloucester	13, 81
Gloucester House	110
Great Western and West Midland Railway	75, 82
Great Western Railways	13
Green Lane	84
Guildhall Worcester	17
Gurneys	61

H

Hay Wines	62
Henwick	81
Heritage Centre	42, 56
Hereford	12, 13, 15, 80
Hereford and Gloucester Canal	73
Herefordshire and Gloucestershire Canal Trust	75
Hereford Basin	75
Herefordshire Council	13
Hereford Journal	74
Hereford Museum and Library Service	73
High Street	10, 25, 33, 61
Hills Yard	32
Hollybush	94
Holts, The	108
Homend	16, 18, 29, 31, 33, 35, 76
Homend Bakery	30
Homend House	36
Homend Walk	34
Horse Lane	96
Horseshoe Inn	38, 115
House on Stilts	64
Humphreys, William	43
Hus Hem	61

I

Ice Bytes	16, 34
Isaacs Linen Shop	37

J

Jenkins Fresh Fruit	38
John de Almeley	48
John Masefield High School	110
Jones, George	4, 58

K

King Stephen	18
Knapp, The	36, 77

L

Lakefest	19
Land Rover Experience	106
Laycock	107
Lay Lines	73
Leadon Valley	79
Leonardo de Vinci	50
Leonardson, Jim	4
Ledbury Books and Maps	15
Ledbury Cycle Hire	14
Ledbury Guardian	33
Ledbury Halt	72, 81
Ledbury Mop Fair	18, 19
Ledbury Parish Church of St Michael and All Angels	48, 84
Ledbury Park also known as New House	33, 59, 65, 89, 96
Ledbury Poetry Festival	18, 57
Ledbury Primary School	57
Ledbury Railway Tunnnel	80
Ledbury Railway Station	68, 77
Ledbury Town Trail	72, 77
Ledbury to Gloucester Railway line	75
Ledbury Town Wharf	72
Ledbury Viaduct	79
Leominster	73
Lion Microbrewery	116
Llandinabo Farm Shop	38
London	14
London Midland Railway Company	12
Lower Cross	89

M

Madders Yard	34
Malvern	11, 13, 81
Malvern Book Cooperative	17
Malvern Gazette	25
Market Theatre	19
Masters House	10, 24, 25, 63, 70
Map Shop	16
Market House	18, 26, 63, 89, 95
Market House Cafe	40
Masefield, Edward	36, 77
Masefield, John	3, 9, 36, 57, 77
Masefield, John Poetry Society	47
Masefield Solicitors	49
Master's House	22, 23
Melrose House	37

Monkhide	75	**P**	
Mrs Muffins Teashop	44	Painted Room, The	42, 88
Muse cafe	39	Peel, Robert	96
		Pevsner Nikolaus	48, 96
		Pictorial Guides of the Malvern Hills	94
N			
Nags Head	35	Plague see Black Death	
National Express	14	Plough Hotel	32
Newent	13, 73, 74	Police Station	97
Newport, Abergavenny & Hereford Railway Company	80	Pope John XXII	24
		Prince of Wales Public House	42, 88, 116
New Street	74		
North Chapel	55	Prince Rupert	65, 96
		Priory Lodge and Priory Gatehouse	59, 97
O		Pytel, Walenty	110
Old Cleeve Churchyard	58		
Old Magistrates House	48, 87	**Q**	
		QR code	5, 56
Old Kitchen Tea Room	107	Queen's Walk	72
Olive Tree Italian Restaurant	30	**R**	
Ordnance Survey map	14, 15	Raft Clothes Shop	44
		Retreat, The Public House	62, 63, 117
Over Junction	81		
Oxenhall	74, 75, 76	River Leadon	11
Oxford, Worcester & Wolverhampton Railway Company	81	River Severn	72, 73
		Ross on Wye	11, 12, 15
		Royal Oak Public House	111, 117

Russell, Thomas	57	St Katherine the Virgin	23
		St Martin of Tours	54
S		Stourport on Severn	73
Savage, Su	7	String factory	71
Serenity Hairdressers	61		
Seven Stars Public House	39, 118		
		T	
Scattergood's yard	30	Talbot, The	33, 66, 119
Scott, Sir George Gilbert	103	Tannery Lane	63
Shanti-Shanti Handicrafts	61	The Field publication	100
Sissons, Justine	7	Thorns Place	34
Skew Bridge	77	Three Counties Bookshop	15
Skipp Alley	30	Three Counties Cider Shop	40
Skinner, Edward	52, 65, 96	Tilley's Alley	60, 62
Skynner, Elizabeth & family	53, 54	Tinsmith Alley	62
Smirk, Robert	27	Tourist Information Centre	16
Smoke Alley also known as Smock Alley	38	Town Council Offices	88
Somers Cox	103		
Somers, Lady of Eastnor	103	**U**	
Southend	110	Underdown	110
Stagecoach	13	Upper Cross	89
St Anne's Chapel	52	Upperfields	82, 83
St John the Baptist Eastnor	101	Upperhall Estate	84
St Katherine's Hospital & car park	10, 22, 23, 26, 27, 64, 70	Upper Road	02

V

Velvet Bean Chocolate Shop	38
Victoria Coach Station	14

W

Walled Garden	48, 84, 85, 87
Waller, DT and Sons	37, 116
Wards Row	36
Wargent, George	85
Waterstones	16
Watkins, Alfred	72
Wellington Inn	119
Westons Cider	120
West Midlands Railway Company	81, 82
White Hart	87
White Horse, The	35
Worcester	12, 13, 16
Wye Valley	15

X

Y

Yarkhill	75
YouTube	6

Z